write it.

How to Move From 'Just Thinking About It' to Actually Finishing Your First Nonfiction Book

Adina Samuels

entrechat

ISBN (paperback): 978-1-0673699-0-3

ISBN (ebook): 978-1-0673699-1-0

Published by Entrechat Press

Toronto, Canada

Cover design by Gary Meyer and Arina Zelenskaya

Edited by Frank and Romi Samuels, and Hannah Brown

Proofread and Formatting by Shelly Zevlever

First edition.

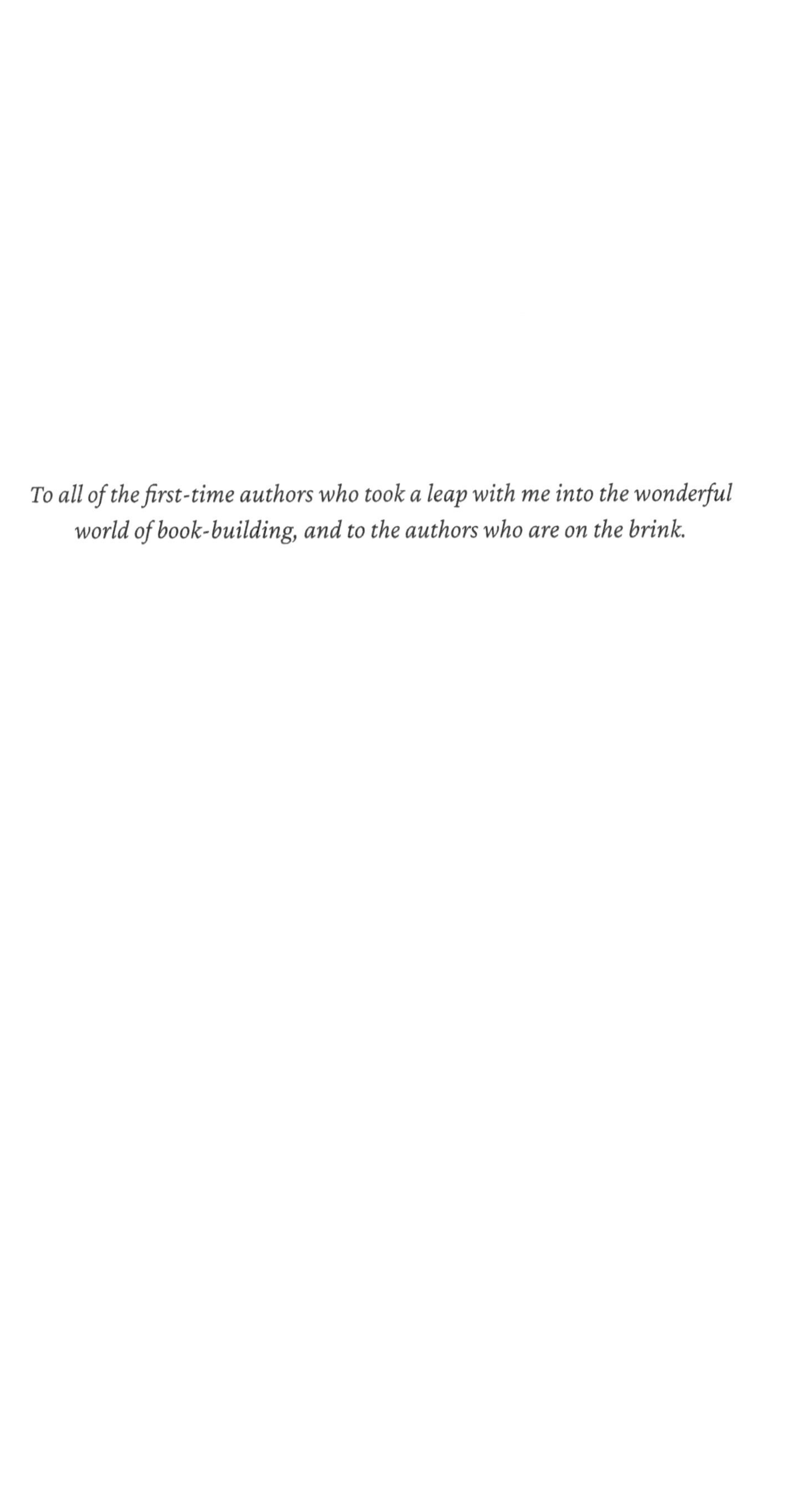

To all of the first-time authors who took a leap with me into the wonderful world of book-building, and to the authors who are on the brink.

Foreword

Adina Samuels does more than teach you how to write a book, she walks beside you and dismantles every excuse that's held you back.

As a coach, she sets herself apart with her warm, irreverent, encouraging but disarmingly honest voice that dispenses with all pretence. Her book opens with a story about a stranger's failed pickup line in a café and somehow turns it into a meditation on courage that follows you through every chapter. Her signature question — What's the worst that could happen? — becomes less of a prompt and more of a compass.

As a coach, Adina understands something most instructional authors miss: the biggest obstacle to writing isn't craft — it's belief. She devotes serious attention to the mental barriers that keep manuscripts trapped in Google Drive, and she does it without a whiff of condescension. When she tells you to "rebrand 'writer' as 'person who writes,'" you feel liberated to enter a creative domain reserved for others.

The practical framework is genuinely useful — from defining your WHY to building a chapter blueprint to a three-pass editing method — but the real value is in how she delivers it. Adina is simultaneously your strategist, your accountability partner, and the friend who won't let you quit. Her "Ghost's Notes" sidebars, where she documents her own doubts and missteps in real time, are a masterclass in leading by example.

This is not a book about writing. It's a book about starting, and finishing, something that scares you. Read it, then open the doc. I did. After completing two books using Adina's methods, expertise, coaching, and motivation, I have moved on to my third. Adina opened a new world of creative expression for me, one that I hadn't dared reduce to an item on a bucket list, but couldn't abandon either.

No more excuses. Write it.

— Orlando Da Silva, LSM Chief Administrator (CEO) of the Administrative Tribunals Support Service of Canada and former President of the Ontario Bar Association

Introduction

The Question That Started It All

There's a café near my apartment where the sunlight hits the tables just right. There's a spinning silver disco ball that refracts the sun's rays into tiny little squares that dance on the walls. Usually, there's American jazz playing. Sometimes it's pop rock. It's also where a lot of this book was written.

One afternoon, I was people watching while sipping on my Americano (single shot, splash of milk) and I saw a young man walk up to a stranger.

"I wrote about you in my gratitude journal," he said, then proceeded to ask her for her number.

She blinked, and politely declined. "I have a boyfriend," she said. He gave a tight-lipped smile, nodded and left. Life went on.

I remember thinking he was incredibly brave. Then I turned to the woman (I just couldn't help myself) and asked, "Do you actually have a boyfriend?"

She laughed. "No. I just thought that was super creepy."

Huh, I thought. So which is it? Brave? Or creepy?

As I watched him walk away, that old question showed up again: *What's the worst that could happen?*

That question is how I ended up here, writing a book for people who want to write books.

I didn't set out to be a book coach, or a ghostwriter, or an independent publisher. Instead, I just listened to this little nagging voice in my head that said "not this" to Teacher's College, and "definitely not that" to law school. So I stuck to what was always a yes to that pesky little voice: reading and writing and listening to the things people had to say.

And then, one day, someone asked me a question.

"Have you ever ghostwritten a book?"

At that point, the answer was no. But I had spent years reading everything I could get my hands on, studying English in university (because novels made more sense to buy than textbooks), interviewing hundreds of people about their passions in an attempt to find mine, hosting a pandemic late-night talk show, and then disappearing to a fishing village in Ghana where I started a travel podcast and shared the stories of the people I met.

Back in Toronto, I took a job producing podcasts for executives across every industry you can imagine: HR, fraud, ethics, change management... (Yes, I can make small talk about anti-money-laundering protocols if pressed.) If a podcast guest had a book, I perked up. I'd order it, underline it, and vet it. Ninety nine percent of the time, a strong book resulted in a strong interview.

So when that early client asked if I could help him tell his story, I said the truest thing I could without lying, "Not a book... yet. But I *can* do this with you."

We spent a year together, meeting weekly, laughing, crying, and coming up with messy drafts. We built his memoir from the ground up. When he paid me to do the thing I loved—researching, interviewing, writing in someone else's voice—I felt like I'd snuck into the best job in the world.

In fact, I thought it was a fluke. Too good to be true. So when the project ended, I turned the page and went back to trying to figure out what, exactly, I was supposed to do with my life.

Hindsight is 20/20, isn't it?!

Then, a few years later, another person came along with a patch-work manuscript that was desperately screaming for help from the first page. We untangled it together, chapter by chapter, and note by note, and turned it into a real book. That book opened doors for him: TV appearances, international stages, new business opportunities. He even put my name on the cover. Again, I thought, *Surely this isn't a career. Surely this is just... nice.*

Meanwhile, life kept nudging me. And, to be clear, by "nudging," I mean that I got fired. Which is a very clarifying nudge, in case you were wondering.

I stumbled into the grips of a business coach for "solopreneurs." I started taking on more authors. I kept reading, kept poking holes in the maze of publishing. I went down printing options and metadata rabbit holes. I got in front of anyone and everyone I could in the industry. The more I learned, the more I realized how much first-time authors were expected to "just know."

Now that we're getting all personal, I'll share with you that I believe I am a relatively anxious and risk-averse individual. Not quite the "jump and the net will appear" type. And yet, despite the fear that came with building a business, I found that writing books with people, building the systems to move them from ideas to chapters to spine-stamped reality just really lit me up. It wasn't anxiety-induc-ing, because the path was just so clear. It didn't feel like a risk. It felt right.

So I built a boutique practice around a simple promise: no gate-keeping. If I learn it, you learn it. If there's a cost, we'll name it. If there's a choice, I'll help you make it.

This book is that promise, written down.

This is not a memoir (though stories you definitely will hear). It's not a "you must do it *this* way" manifesto. This is my attempt at creating a path for you so you can go from *I think I have something to say* to *here's my manuscript, and here's what it will do for my life and work.*

We're going to start with the beliefs that quietly sabotage your best intentions. We'll dismantle each one and replace them with micro actions you can take to prove your inner voice wrong.

Then we'll dig into your WHY. This is the only thing strong enough to carry you through the inevitable *I'd-rather-clean-my-sock-drawer-than-write-another-word* days.

From there, you'll set your compass (your WHAT). Then I'll show you how to build a book with a blueprint that basically becomes your bible. You'll choose your path, and map your chapters so you never sit down thinking *now what?* when it comes to your writing. We'll make realistic goals based on a rhythm that survives bad sleep and busy weeks, and we'll build systems that protect your attention so even the best reels on TikTok won't get in your way.

We'll edit in stages, and I'll show you exactly how to work with an editor so the partnership makes your book sharper.

And if you're thinking, *But what if I mess it up? What if I start and stall? What if I'm not ready?* Just ask yourself my favorite question: What's the worst that could happen?

A messy paragraph?

A draft you outgrow?

No! Stop! The horror! The horror!

Now, instead, I want you to try this. Ask yourself: what's the best that could happen?

You put words to something your readers have been feeling for years.

You unlock opportunities you can't yet predict, like speaking invitations, new clients, partnerships, and a deeper sense of your own voice.

You leave something durable behind.

I can't promise this will be easy. (It shouldn't be.) But I can promise you won't do it alone.

Consider me your pushy flight attendant. I'll wake you when you doze off, get you to where you need to go, and feed you the occasional stale croissant with a lukewarm coffee.

So, pull up a chair. Open the doc. Take a breath.

Let's write the book only *you* can write.

What's the worst that could happen?

A Note Before We Begin

This is a Live Experiment... Results Pending

THIS ISN'T JUST a book *about* writing a book.

This is a book that's being written in real time, using the exact strategies I offer within it.

As you read these chapters, know that I'm doing the exact same things I'm asking you to do. I'm outlining, drafting, and editing alongside you.

You'll see my process woven throughout: what worked, what didn't, and what I wish I'd known sooner.

Basically, I'm trying to make all the mistakes so you don't have to.

Some of these reflections will appear as sidebars where I'll share behind-the-scenes moments from my own journey.

They'll look a little something like this:

The Ghost's Notes

Hi, it's me! I'm the Ghost :)

Others will live online, where I'll post updates, data, and real outcomes.

If you want to follow along in real time, find me on LinkedIn! You'll get access to monthly updates about how this book finds its readers (and maybe how I recover from the inevitable missteps). It's basically the "director's commentary" version of this project.

My goal is to show you that this process is one hundred percent ready-to-use.

I'm inviting you to do as I do, and as I say. How could I tell you to do something I haven't done myself?!

Here we go.

On AI and Authorship

Let's just take a quick second to acknowledge the world we're writing in.

Right now, you could open a new tab, type a few prompts into an AI tool, and have an entire book draft in minutes.

Pretty wild, isn't it?

You don't need to wrestle with structure, stare at a blinking cursor, or survive caffeine-fueled spirals wondering if a comma should be a semicolon or a period instead.

Talk about productivity!

If your goal is purely to create a product, AI can definitely do a lot of that work for you.

There's nothing wrong with that, either. It's efficient, scalable, and, for some authors, perfectly aligned with their purpose.

But those aren't usually the authors I work with.

The people I tend to attract are writing from somewhere a little deeper. They're creating from a sense of purpose or curiosity. They often have a desire to help, to teach, to make a difference, or to leave something durable behind.

For these kinds of authors, AI likely won't cut it.

Take a second and engage in this thought experiment with me for a second:

If the world were ending in thirty days and you wanted to write a book, would you ask AI to write it for you or would you want to write it yourself, even if no one else ever read it?

If your answer is *I'd want to write it myself,* then you're exactly who this book is for. See, that impulse to create even when no one's watching is the seed of every meaningful book.

If your answer is AI, that's okay too. There are other guides out there that will teach you how to produce a book quickly and efficiently. This just isn't one of them.

This book is for those in it for the long haul.

Are you?

The Ghost's Notes

I know, I know. The robots are here, and they're not leaving. So if you can't beat 'em, learn to use 'em, right?

I'm with you! In fact, there are great ways to bring AI into your process for brainstorming, outlining, organizing research, and testing marketing ideas. But before you let AI draft for you, pause and revisit that question I asked earlier. If the world was ending, would you still want to write it yourself?

That answer will keep you grounded during those late night moments when you wonder why you ever started this project in the first place. (More on your WHY soon.)

Faulty Beliefs

The Stories We Tell Ourselves

The Ghost's Notes

Many people think they're not creative, but if they listened to their own inner voice for five minutes, they'd have to take that back.

Humans are wildly *imaginative, just usually in the wrong direction.*

Let me explain.

We invent elaborate stories about why something won't work, rationalize every risk away, and twist reality into a neat little safety blanket.

It's brilliant, really. Our brains evolved to protect us from lions in the jungle. But in modern life, those same defence mechanisms mostly just keep us from starting.

Instead, what we need to do is break through those thought patterns and lean into the fear and uncertainty. I guarantee there are no lions along for this ride (unless you've got an especially unique memoir to write.)

THE FIRST TIME I seriously thought about writing my own book, I lasted about... five minutes. I opened a blank document, stared at the cursor, and immediately thought: *Who am I kidding? I'm not a real author.*

Sound familiar?

From the hundreds of conversations I've had with new authors, it has become abundantly clear to me that the main thing stopping them from getting started isn't their packed schedules, or their areas of expertise.

The thing that stops most people is their beliefs.

I've watched brilliant and capable leaders stall on their manuscripts because they were tangled up in myths that were stopping them from even giving it a try.

Maybe you've thought some of these, too:

"I'm not an author."

"My story isn't important enough."

"I'll never be able to actually finish this thing."

What do these statements have in common?

None of them is fact. These are just your fears. And they're also the number one reason books that could change lives never make it past someone's Google Drive.

So before we talk about structure or publishing or marketing, we're going to start here: with the stories you tell yourself.

But Adina, I'm not into this woo-woo stuff. Can I skip this part?

Sure, you can. But I will say that one thing I've learned over and over again is that more than half of your success comes from your mindset. If you're cringing just reading that, I was like that too! But then I read *Think and Grow Rich* and *The 5AM Club* and *The 7 Habits of Highly Effective People* and I realized that this is what propels some of the biggest business minds of our time. Thinking you can do it is maybe more than half the battle! Our subconscious needs it.

In fact, my business coach Moe Choice forced me to spend a WEEK determining things like my "purpose," my "principles," and my "goals." I was desperate for strategies and templates, but he stopped me. "This first, Adina," he said. "How you talk to your subconscious is the thing that matters the most." It was very much a Mr. Miyagi moment.

Once you get this part straight and learn to work *with* your mind instead of against it, the process of writing a book suddenly feels a lot less intimidating... and a lot more possible.

Here's more from Moe:

"Milton H. Erickson, the godfather of hypnosis, said that the only reason people seek therapy is because their conscious and their subconscious are out of alignment. My version of that is that if you're not fully aligned with the nonconscious part of you, you'll never be able to live life on your own terms."

Did we sell ya? I hope so. Let's begin.

<u>The Ghost's Notes</u>
Curious about the mindset and subconscious stuff?

Check out these books, recommended by Moe himself:
"The Chimp Paradox" by Steve Peters
"Incognito: The Secret Lives of the Brain" by David Eagleman
"The Power of Your Subconscious Mind" by Joseph Murphy
"Thinking, Fast and Slow" by Daniel Kahneman

The Faulty Beliefs

Faulty Belief 1: "I'm Not a Writer"

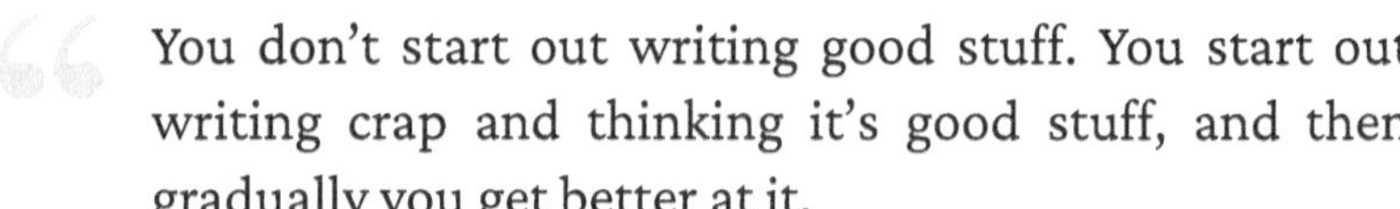

> You don't start out writing good stuff. You start out writing crap and thinking it's good stuff, and then gradually you get better at it.

— Octavia E. Butler

I CAN'T TELL you how many times I've stared at a blank page and thought: *Well, that's it. The jig is up. I am officially not a writer. They're all going to know now.*

I've also heard this from dozens of clients. "I can't do this. I'm not a writer."

But what does that even mean? Do we really think "real writers" sit down and pour out brilliance in a single draft? *(They don't.)*

Do we think they never need editors or accountability? *(They all do.)*

Do we believe you need a degree in literature before you're

allowed to put words on a page? (*Absolutely not...but don't tell 18-year-old me that. She loved her Victorian poetry classes in those drafty old churches with the stained-glass windows.*)

If being "a writer" means producing perfect pages from the start, then no one among us is or has ever been a writer.

James Clear, in *Atomic Habits,* says it well: "Every action you take is a vote for the type of person you wish to become."

That means writing a single messy paragraph is a vote. Hitting your weekly word count is another vote. Sitting down to try again is another vote.

You act into the person you want to be. You aren't born into it.

I've seen this play out again and again with my first-time authors.

As you allow yourself to begin, your ideas get sharper the moment they hit the page. Then, your confidence grows as you see words stack up week after week. Soon after, people around you start to notice: "Oh, she's the one writing a book." Suddenly, you're the go-to voice in your field.

And eventually, you realize that you don't have to *be* a writer to write a book. You become one by writing.

See, the fear of "not being a writer" is completely backwards.

You don't wait until you're a writer to start. You start, and that's what makes you a writer.

Mic drop.

So here's my question: if you sat down today and wrote 500 messy words, would that make you "not a writer"... or the exact opposite?

A little exercise:

Think of three small actions you could do this week that prove you *are* someone who writes.

The Ghost's Notes

I found this excerpt in my notes folder, back when I was knee-deep in my quarter life crisis:

When do I get to call myself a writer?

Is it once my name is in print?

Once thousands of copies of my writing have been sold?

Once I've got a by-line?

Once my LinkedIn profile says so?

Or do all the years of keeping journals count? What about the countless notes on my phone, writing my thoughts and reflecting on the world? Or the scraps of paper, napkins, backs of checks, and tax forms?

Little did she know she was a writer this whole time! She just hadn't voted for herself yet.

Faulty Belief 2: "I Don't Have Time to Write a Book"

> You don't need to find time to write. You need to make time. That's the difference.
>
> — Toni Morrison

The most common thing people tell me when they flirt with the idea of writing a book is this: *"I just don't have the time."*

I've said the same thing myself. See, I'm not great at *downtime*. A typical day for me includes early mornings at the gym and working on the business, then ceramics classes, volleyball league, language exchange, community choir… you get the idea. My days often feel full before they've even started.

As an aside, I find Saturdays and Sundays to be my favorite days for working. A whole day, without a single meeting? Endless time to check things off my to-do list? That's my personal form of paradise.

But here's what most people don't recognize: If you zoom out and really look at how much time writing a book takes, it's shockingly… not that crazy.

One of my clients, Ron, felt that massive sense of overwhelm about halfway through his book. He's a busy man. His schedule is packed with speaking engagements, networking opportunities, further education, family time… He and I are cut from the same cloth!

When he came my way, he was half-convinced that his schedule was too packed to make any progress and he was doubting whether the book was a good idea. But then he made a choice with himself. His book was enough of a priority that he promised himself that he'd spend 30 minutes per day, laptop open, even if that meant he did it at 10pm. It was a non-negotiable. That single choice turned into a habit, and that habit turned into a finished book.

That's all it took. Sheer will, persistence, and the promise to himself.

I know that when people imagine themselves writing a book, they picture six months in a wooden cabin with nothing but a typewriter and black coffee. Ideally with a lake to look at, too.

But that is so absolutely NOT what it takes to write your book! In fact, some of my most productive writing sessions are in the most unlikely of places (bustling airports, train stops, or hostel lounges). Why? Because my purpose SURPASSES my external environment.

Now, I wouldn't turn down a romantic escape to the woods, but it's certainly not essential.

What will really get you to the finish line is this: small and consistent sessions stacked up over time.

Greg McKeown, author of *Essentialism,* says this, "If you don't prioritize your life, someone else will."

The same goes for your book. If you don't prioritize it—even in tiny doses—it will never magically "fit in."

Finishing a book doesn't require endless hours. It's much simpler than that. All you need is:

C: Clear structure so you know exactly what to write each week.

R: Realistic writing rhythm (even just 500 words, 3-4 times a week).

A: Accountability to keep you honest.

F: Feedback + editing to make the messy parts readable.

T: Tangible milestones so you can celebrate progress along the way.

That's it.

Those are also all the elements that this book offers. Huh. Talk about a useful resource!

So I ask you this (like I ask all my hesitant clients): *Do you really think committing to 1,000 words a week for 6–9 months will wreck your calendar?*

What's your answer?

Of course it won't wreck your calendar! In fact, I've always believed that if you want something done, ask the busiest person to do it.

Let that be you for this next chapter of your life.

Embrace and prioritize this journey. Soon you'll come to look forward to the time you've locked away just for you and your book.

So, are you going to let the myth of "no time" stop you? Or are you ready to carve out a little space each week for the book that could change everything?

Remember, you really only need a few hours. If you can make time for ratting out your neighbor for not separating his recycling from his green bin, then I think you can carve out some time for this.

A little exercise for you to try:

Pick one consistent block of time this week. This could be first thing in the morning, or during a lunch break. Even late nights work. Just dedicate that block to writing. Treat it like Ron did: a standing appointment with yourself.

<u>The Ghost's Notes</u>

Pri·or·i·ty: the fact or condition of being regarded or treated as more important.

A lot of people talk about priorities (plural). But that is actually a contradictory thing to say, if you think about it.

The very word priority is SINGULAR, meaning you can only have one thing that is a true priority.

The belief of not having enough time will be enough to stop you if you have a whole boatload of competing priorities.

You need to prioritize your book the same way you would a romantic relationship, or the goal of running a marathon.

You can make all the excuses for not texting back, or sleeping in when you should be on mile 6, but in reality, you were the only thing getting in your own way.

One more thing: Writing a book should be something you WANT to make time for, too. This should not just be another thing to tick off your to-do list. Your book needs your passion!

Faulty Belief 3: "I Don't Know If I Have Something Worth Writing"

There is no greater agony than bearing an untold story inside you.

— Maya Angelou

"Adina, is what I have to say really worth sharing? I haven't climbed Everest or survived some dramatic life-or-death thing. Who's going to care?"

I hear this a lot, which is fair.

But the worst kind of book is the one that tries to please everyone.

If you want to write something people *love*, that automatically means some people won't connect with it, or may even dismiss it.

As a people pleaser, the concept of someone dismissing my work makes me shudder. Heck, when I get a contrasting opinion on a LinkedIn post, I question my very existence.

But, just as I remind myself, I will tell you too.

Writing your story and having people engage with it (even enough to say "no thanks, not interested")... that in itself is *proof* you're saying something that matters.

In *This Is Marketing*, Seth Godin calls this finding your "smallest viable audience." You're searching for the smallest group of people who can sustain your work, and on the journey, you'll find those who want to come along for the ride, and those who do not.

A "good book" isn't one that makes everyone nod politely. That's like trying to be best friends with every single person at a networking event. I've tried it, I promise. All I end up with is a bloated stomach from eating one too many chicken skewers, and barely a single meaningful conversation.

The books that actually change people are the ones that make some readers think, *"Finally, someone said what I've been feeling."* And yes, they also make others think, *"Not for me."*

Both of these responses are helpful. Let me explain why:

When a reader feels seen, they become your biggest fan and share your book. That's easy to conceptualize.

And when a reader doesn't connect, they step aside, leaving you with an audience who truly resonates. Even if they leave a mean comment on your Instagram, all it takes is you to turn off your phone for an hour and the sting resides! Plus, all publicity is good publicity, right?

I consulted a good friend of mine, Mike, on this very issue, as he was starting his digital content business.

His audience spent most of their time on Reddit, and, as he explained to me, Reddit can be a very dark and scary place. All those mean internet trolls really know how to twist the knife deep.

But despite the fear, he did the scary thing anyway. Now, his business is taking off, with the right people giving him attention, and he's never looked back.

Similarly, when your book takes a stance, it sparks conversation, curiosity, and connection. These are the very things that make books spread.

Try out this reframe (say it with me):

- My book will be meaningful if I tell the story only I can tell.
- My book will be meaningful for the right readers, and no one else. And that is enough.
- My book will not be meaningful if it appeals to everyone.
- Every book that's ever mattered has had its critics. But it also had champions. Those champions are who I'm writing for.

So stop asking if your story is "enough." The fact that you're even wrestling with that question means you already have something worth writing! Do you see that yet?

Try this out:

List 5 people (real or imagined) who might need to hear your story in your words. Write one sentence about why it would matter to each of them.

<u>The Ghost's Notes</u>
Here's me talking to me as much as I'm talking to you: rejection or indifference isn't the end of the world. It's part of the process.

I spent three years as a podcast producer, chasing guests to come on the show. At one point I tracked my "success" rate. I think it sat at a meager 5%. Meaning, 95% of my job was expecting people to say no to me.

It's the same with my business now!

But, over time that rejection makes you stronger! Now, I have no fear walking up to someone and telling them I wrote about them in my gratitude journal… I think. I haven't actually tried that one out yet.

Do I dare?!

Faulty Belief 4: "I Need to Have It All Figured Out Before I Start"

 You can't edit a blank page.

— Jodi Picoult

This belief goes something like, *"I can't start writing until I know exactly how the whole book will turn out."*

Wait—you mean you expect to map out the entire journey before taking a single step? That's like planting a seed, checking the next morning for a tree, and deciding gardening just doesn't work.

The Ghost's Notes

This one is familiar to me, too. I'm the kind of person who's had things come fairly easily to me. I never had to study too hard, it never took too long for me to understand a concept.

And then came eleventh grade Advanced Functions. Boy, did I get a reality check then! The formulas just weren't formula-ing. I found myself stuck, over and over again.

If I could have, I probably would have given up. "Not for me," I'd say, and slither away from any and all trace of vectors and parabolas.

Unfortunately for me, dropping the course was not an option. So I had to lean all the way in. It hurt, let me tell you. Just thinking back to it now, I still feel the same pang I did on Monday mornings before class.

Eventually, though, I surrendered to the idea of not knowing the answer, or not understanding the concepts right away. And thanks to some late-night tutoring sessions and good friends helping me out, I aced the course! Woo!

Same thing here.

I promise you that no author IN HISTORY has had it all figured out before they started.

Every single book begins as a messy and uncertain draft. Even the most successful authors will tell you that their first attempts were clunky, half-baked, and full of holes. The clarity only came *through* writing, not before.

In *Think Again,* Adam Grant talks about the power of rethinking. He explains how our best ideas often emerge after we've tested, revised, and reworked them.

Books are no different. You don't think your way into the perfect outline. You write your way into it.

And, just like eventually I started to anticipate what a bi-convex parabola should look like, you'll get better at this as you go along.

So, to repeat: you do not need to know all the answers!

Waiting until you "know everything" will guarantee only one thing: paralysis.

Give in to the magic and let it grow as you grow into the process.

Take Fred, for example.

When we met, Fred knew he wanted to write a book. He had a number of principles floating around in his head, and plenty of stories to tell. But he had no idea how he wanted to tell his story.

It took us about a month of just getting to know each other, chatting and learning, for me to even give him a useful proposal of what I thought his book could look like.

Throughout all of this time, he was under no pressure, and fully believed in the process. He didn't need to know what "the end" looked like. He was just existing in the present, putting one step after the other. And, it worked. As soon as we aligned, he was full speed ahead on his book. (Unsurprisingly, one of his principles is all about focusing on outputs, not outcomes.)

So here's my nudge! This is it! It's time to stop waiting for the perfect plan. You don't need to have it all figured out before you start. You just need to start.

Try this out:

Sit down and write one messy page: stream-of-consciousness, no editing, no outline.

One rule: Don't stop until you fill the page.

This will show you how clarity comes *through* writing, not before. And if no clarity comes, come back to it tomorrow. The clarity will eventually need somewhere to release itself. Give it the chance.

Faulty Belief 5: "Everything I Want to Say Has Already Been Written"

> There are only two or three human stories, and they go on repeating themselves as fiercely as if they had never happened before.
>
> — Willa Cather

I can't tell you how many times I've heard this one: *"Why should I write a book? Other people have already written about leadership / resilience / grief / entrepreneurship / insert your topic here."*

And every time, I ask: why would someone else's book cancel out yours?

Someone else writing about burnout doesn't erase *your* lived experience of it. Another founder publishing a book on scaling a company doesn't diminish the fact that *you* built a business, with your own wins, losses, and lessons along the way.

Austin Kleon, in *Steal Like an Artist,* puts it like this, "Every new idea is just a mashup or remix of one or more previous ideas."

In other words, there's nothing new under the sun.

In other *other words,* originality isn't the point. It can't be, because you won't get there. No one will.

So if originality isn't the point, what is?

Enter the power of resonance.

You know when you're talking to a therapist, and they say something to you and you just go—"Yes! Exactly! That is exactly what I mean!" That is resonance. And it is powerful.

Readers don't care whether you invented the idea. They care whether your perspective helps them, or makes them see something differently.

So no, your book won't be dismissed because others have written on the topic.

In fact, you'd much rather be known as *"the leader who finally put words to what I've been struggling with"* than be absent from the bookshelf because you convinced yourself your story didn't count.

Want proof? Think about all the books you've read on similar themes—memoirs of loss, business guides, personal growth. Did you ever toss them aside saying, *"Eh, this has already been written"*? Or did you underline passages, see yourself in the pages, and feel grateful that the author chose to share their version?

That's exactly what your readers will feel when they read yours.

So let me ask you: whose life might change because they heard the story in *your* words, at *your* time, in *your* voice?

Try this:

Go to your bookshelf (or library, or Kindle) and pull 3 books on similar themes. Go on, I'll wait.

For each, jot down what made you feel connected. Notice also that just because they all have the same themes, they all found a space on your shelf.

<u>The Ghost's Notes</u>
On a slightly philosophical note, I used to often wonder about why each of us has to learn the same lessons over and over again, generation after generation.

Why must I also suffer the pangs of heartbreak if those who have come before me have already healed their scars? Why can't evolution just catch up, so I can skip the painful bits?

But that's the whole point, isn't it?

We're meant to live the stories ourselves. We can't go through life just reading about them. We are here to feel them, learn from them, and tell them in our own way.

Your book is part of that continuum. Yes, it is a sort of retelling. But this is one the world hasn't heard quite like this before.

Faulty Belief 6: "I Can Do This Completely On My Own"

 Writing is a lonely job. Having someone who believes in you makes a lot of difference. They don't have to make speeches. Just believing is usually enough.

— Stephen King

"I don't need help writing my book. I'll just sit down and do it myself."

Sure. And I could technically cut my own bangs too—but we all know how that ends.

(Don't believe me? Try scrolling through my Facebook profile picture circa 2014...)

If writing a book only required brute force, the Spartans would be remembered for their memoirs instead of their military strategy.

Writing isn't meant to be a solo act of survival. It's not you versus the blank page. And when you treat it like that, then you'll just end up in a battle against yourself.

I recommend you think of writing a book less like going to war and more like raising a child. Could you do it alone? Technically, yes. But it's a lot easier when someone shows up with a casserole, a bottle of wine, and a "You're doing great, sweetie."

I think all authors need some version of that. So, when writing your book, say yes to help. I promise it doesn't make you less of a writer.

What help might you need?

You may need help with structure, and preparing the page before you dig in to the writing.

You may need a sounding board to play with some of your ideas.

You might need someone to shake you out of a stupor when it feels like you've hit a wall.

You definitely need at least one new pair of eyes on your work before sending it off to print.

In *Mindset,* Carol Dweck writes about the difference between a fixed mindset ("I should be able to do this alone") and a growth mindset ("I can get better with support").

This is the kind of approach we need to take with our book babies.

The Ghost's Notes

Okay, I have a bit of a controversial take on Mindset.

It's a good book, sure, but it's basically one core idea dressed in a hundred different examples.

So. Many. Examples.

By chapter five, I found myself thinking, Yes, Carol, I get it.
And yet, 3 million copies sold. It's a corporate training staple and Dweck is undoubtedly a household name.

Why?

We'll come back to this when we talk about structure, but, in short:

While I might roll my eyes at the repetition, it's also exactly what made the book a bestseller.

One clear memorable idea repeated across experiences is often far more powerful than a complex one explained once.

So, just like hiring a babysitter doesn't make you any less of a parent, getting a second opinion or bouncing ideas off of a thought partner doesn't take away from you being an author.

That leaves me with a question: who is in your corner?

And if your answer is no one–well, that's not entirely true.

I'm right here. (Hi!)

You can think of this book as your first writing partner.

Try this:

Draw a quick map of the people and resources you could lean on: a coach, a writing buddy, an editor, even a friend who asks "How's the book going?"

Label where you already have support, and where you might need to add it.

Smashing Through
the Faulty Beliefs

By now, you've played all of the greatest hits of self-doubt:

CUE THE INTRO THEME:

"I'm not a writer."

"I don't have time."

"I don't know if my story matters."

(and a few more cult favorites that sound suspiciously like excuses).

So let's flip the script. Here are some simple and tangible ways to smash through those beliefs and actually start writing your book:

Rebrand "Writer" as "Person Who Writes": You don't have to wait for a magical title to be bestowed upon you. Write one paragraph, and you're already a person who writes. Done.

Steal Time, Don't Wait for It: You don't "find" time, you make it. One of my clients, Ron, finished his book by writing at Starbucks for just an hour each morning before work.

Write First, Figure It Out Later: Jodi Picoult said it best: *"You can't edit a blank page."* So, start messy. Let clarity come through the writing, not before.

Stop Aiming for Everyone: Ultimately, there are only a handful of human stories. Yours will resonate with the right people when you're specific. Ask yourself: *Who needs to hear this in my words?*

Don't Go It Alone: Writing a book is a team effort. Seek out feedback, accountability, and encouragement.

Remember: these beliefs don't disappear on their own. You have to *act your way* out of them. Tiny steps, consistent progress, and a little bit of humor go a long way.

So, what's one small action you could take this week to prove yourself wrong?

The Ghost's Notes

I can't stress enough here that the stakes in this situation are VERY LOW.

So you write a chapter, and you hate it. No one ever has to know.

Worst case, you've spent a few hours getting to know the voice inside your head. We could all likely use a little more time with whoever that character is.

Writing is one of the safest ways to stand up to your fears.
Let this be your proof of capability, not to anyone else, but to yourself.

Because, (and say it with me now), what's the worst thing that could happen?

What's Next?

Okay, so we've dragged all those faulty beliefs out into the light, poked holes in them, and (hopefully) had a laugh or two along the way.

It should now be clear that you don't need to wait until you've "fixed" every fear before you start writing. You just need to recognize these beliefs for what they are: stories you've been telling yourself.

Now you can replace them with actions that actually move you forward.

If this isn't yet clear, send me a message with "STILL AFRAID" in the subject line. We'll get to the root of what's in your way.

Next comes the part I love most: figuring out your **WHY.**

We're going to dig deep into why you're really writing this book. Not the surface-level "it would be nice to have" reason. The real reason. The one that's going to keep you coming back to the page when the excitement wears off.

No time like the present! Read on, future writer!

Your WHY

 He who has a why to live can bear almost any how.

— Friedrich Nietzsche

WHY DO we do anything at all? What is the point?

I used to spend a lot of time mulling over this question. I *could* just stay in bed, read my books and drink tea. Why must I face the cold mean world that waits outside my door? The world would continue, time would keep moving, and what would be the point of doing anything else?

One of my authors experiences intense depression. On one of our calls, I asked him why he kept fighting. What made the agony worth it?

He didn't give me some philosophical answer about purpose or meaning. No. He said,"I just want to see what happens at the end of the movie."

That's the best answer I've ever gotten to this question.

Some people are moved by purpose, a sense of something greater, like they're playing some part in a bigger story.

Sometimes I feel like that, too. Certainly more so when things are going my way.

But, I think humans also have this innate curiosity, and a kind of insatiable hope that just won't die. Even when we're confronted by the worst, we go on.

So, all that is to say your "why" can be anything, so long as it is true to you.

Maybe you're writing a book to reflect on what you've learned over 30 years of leadership.

Maybe you're writing a book so that your grandkids will have the chance to get to know you better.

Maybe you're writing a book so that you'll have the chance to get to know yourself better.

There's no wrong "why." It just has to ring true for you.

This isn't only the case for new authors.

Think about marathon runners. Most of them will tell you that at mile 20, everything is telling you to give up. What gets people through is the reason they're running in the first place.

The WHY carries them farther than their muscles alone.

But, please don't ask me too much more about running—my treadmill has officially fired me.

On any arduous journey, the excitement and adventure wears off. It just does. And in those moments of pouring rain and desperation, the thing that will carry you through is your conviction.

Your WHY is what turns "someday I'll write a book" into "I wrote one."

Moving forward, we're going to dig into:

- The return on investment (ROI) of a book
- Defining your WHY with clarity (using the 5 Whys exercise)
- Understanding who you're writing for

By the end of this section, you should have the conviction you need to carry through with your book. And maybe a new pair of running shoes... because if you can train for a marathon you'll never run, you can definitely train for a book you *will* write.

Ready? Let's find your WHY.

The ROI of a Book

W‌HEN I FIRST STARTED THE business, I'd get on tons of discovery calls. If anyone expressed the tiniest glimmer of interest in writing a book, I'd jump on the chance to talk to them.

One of those calls went like this:

"I'm a businessman," he started.

I nodded. Cool. Same.

"I need to know the ROI here. Why should I work with you instead of AI?"

He spoke for almost ten minutes before I could get a word in.

When I finally could, I told him, "I don't think I'm the ghost-writer for you."

See, in my eyes, the purpose of a book is not "quick returns." If that's his modus operandi, he'd likely be very disappointed working with me.

Yes, there are ways a book can bring in new opportunities, but if profit is the only metric, I'd recommend buying a laundromat. (They seem to be having a real renaissance these days.)

In short, the return on investment of a book cannot just be about book sales.

Yes, royalties can be nice. But unless you're Michelle Obama or Colleen Hoover, the real value of your book won't be a check from Amazon. Sorry to break it to you!

The real ROI is the *doors it opens.*

Here are some things to keep in mind when you're building your why:

A book makes prospects lean in. It's easier to trust someone with 200 pages of published thinking than with a LinkedIn headline alone. I know this from experience vetting podcast guests. Potential guests with a book had a much higher chance of getting a slot.

Event organizers love authors. They make for instant credibility in a bio. So if you're looking to do more speaking, a book is a good idea. Reporters look for experts with something substantial behind them. A book makes you quotable.

These are all decent reasons, and common ones. But then there's also this abstract concept of *legacy.* This one's harder to measure, but it resonates with most of my authors. A book lives far beyond a viral post or keynote. It's a body of work your kids or your clients can hold in their hands. If I were to return to my more naive anti-capitalist university days (if you know, you know), I might say this is really the only ROI that matters.

Seth Godin calls books "time machines." They carry your ideas into the future, spreading them farther than you can by yourself. I'd add to this and say that, while they carry your ideas into the future, they bring your reader back to your present, and their past. They transcend time.

So yes, sales are one form of ROI. But if you stop there, I think you might be missing the bigger picture. In fact, if sales is your only ROI, then I do recommend you go ahead and use AI to write your book. I'm curious what kind of sales numbers you get!

Exercise: Book ROI Brainstorm

1. What would make this book a "success" for me, beyond sales?
2. Which doors do I want this book to open? (Credibility? Media? Clients? Speaking?)
3. Who do I most want this book to impact?

Remember: there's no wrong answer here! But when you're clear on the ROI that matters to *you*, it's a lot easier to keep showing up at the page.

<u>The Ghost's Notes</u>

I started writing a novel almost 5 years ago now. I had this urge to just get it out. For months, I wrote like a woman possessed.

Then life crept in—emails, deadlines, the usual—and the novel slowly sank to the bottom of my to-do list.

Now, I have a 20k word draft just sitting somewhere in the recesses of my Google Drive. Why? Because my "why" wasn't strong enough.

I think my "why" then was "because I want to." But when other wants came to compete, my book lost.

It's so much harder now for me to pick up where I left off and try to finish that novel. I'm probably not even the same person I was when I started writing it.

So, your why has to be strong enough to outlast life's interruptions. Otherwise, your draft becomes a time capsule for a version of you that never finished.

Defining Your WHY

 The unexamined life is not worth living.

— Socrates

THE ANCIENT GREEK PHILOSOPHER SOCRATES had a teaching style that drove people a little bit crazy: he never gave straight answers. Instead, he asked questions. Then, he asked more questions. And then, even more, until his students went from surface-level responses to the deeper truths hiding underneath.

He was like a relentless five-year-old driving his poor parents insane. Or, like me on a ghostwriting interview call.

But his teaching style stuck, and became known as the Socratic method. He had figured out a way to help people determine what they really meant, instead of hiding behind the words they chose to use.

When it comes to your book, the same principle applies. You can't stop at "I want to write a book because it would be nice." That's like giving Socrates your first shallow answer. He would've tilted his head, squinted, and said, *"But why?"*

And then when you answered, he'd ask *"Why?"* again. And again. And again.

That's how you can get to the real reason.

<u>The Ghost's Notes</u>

Let's try it out with this book. Here's me having a dialogue with, well, me.

Me: "So, Adina, why do you want to write this book?"

Me (again): "Well, I felt like I was giving a whole lot of advice to my authors without actually having taken a lot of it myself."

Me: "Huh, okay. So what? Why did that mean you needed to write a book?"

Me (again): "Well, credibility, for one. But, I also build relationships based on trust with each of my clients. I couldn't offer them advice in good conscience without knowing it could work."

Me: "Mmm, I see. Interesting. Why, though?"

Me (again): "I wouldn't feel like I was doing good work. I want to give my best to my clients, so they know as much as I do, and can make informed decisions throughout the creation of their book."

Me: Why is "no gatekeeping" your hill to die on?

Me (again): I know how foggy publishing can be. I want to make the path clear and accessible."

Me: "Once again, why does this matter to you?"

Me (again): "The work I get to do is an honor and a privilege. I don't take the responsibility of helping other people share their stories lightly."

Distilled WHY: *I am writing this book to make the path from idea to finished nonfiction transparent and achievable, so first-time authors can own their stories with confidence and make informed decisions at every step.*

Interesting dialogue, huh? See the drop from "credibility" to "no gatekeeping" to "meaningful work"? That's how we go from goal to truth.

Now it's your turn.

Exercise: The 5 Whys

1. Write down your first answer to this question: *"Why do I want to write this book?*
2. Then ask yourself: *"Why does that matter?"* Write the answer.
3. Repeat this five times, each time digging a layer deeper.

Before you begin:

Your first answer will almost always be about external things, like credibility, sales, or visibility. By the third or fourth "why," you'll usually stumble onto something more personal. Maybe legacy, self-trust, healing, or impact. And by the fifth, you'll know if you've hit gold, because the answer will feel less like a goal and more like a truth. You might even get goosebumps.

That's your WHY.

Once you have it, you'll stop worrying about whether you "feel" like writing on any given day. You'll write because the reason matters too much not to.

Who Is Your Book For?

"I WANT my book to reach business executives... but also MBA students. And their parents. And also people who don't usually read books."

In other words: *everyone and their dog.*

The problem with this approach is that a book written for everyone ends up not really speaking to anyone.

You want your readers to experience that almost-spooky feeling that this book is speaking directly to *them.* We're talking as targeted as Amazon ads. (How did Bezos know I was looking for pink furry earmuffs?)

It was the same for me when I was building my business. My coach (Moe, again), forced me to niche down. Once I chose who I was targeting, my offer, my voice, and my messaging became much clearer. It will be the same for your book, too.

Here's what I mean:

It would be one thing if I were to write a book for anyone who's ever thought about writing a book.

It's another to say: This book is for first-time nonfiction authors who want a clear roadmap from manuscript to market.

Angela Duckworth does this well in *Grit*. She hones in on educators, parents, and professionals interested in resilience. (No wonder it all went over my head when I first read it as a lazy fourteen year old–it wasn't for that version of me.) The clarity of her readership is what gave the book staying power, and explains why it became a staple in schools and workplaces.

Now, I know what you might be thinking.

"But, Adina, my book really is for everyone!"

Nope. If you try to please everyone, you water it down so much that no one connects deeply. The strange truth is that the more specific your audience, the broader your impact can be. A book that feels laser-focused for *someone* ends up resonating with *many*.

"Won't narrowing my reader base cut people out?"

It will. But that's actually a *good* thing. Specificity will create loyal readers and followers. These are high-value consumers that can be worth far more than a broadly semi-engaged readership.

"Can't I just figure out my reader later?"

You could, but you'll likely end up rewriting half your book. Your "who" shapes everything, from the stories you tell to the language you use. It also makes publishing, cover design, and marketing 100x easier if you know this in advance. A further note on why this matters NOW:

Your "who" doesn't just help with the writing bit. It becomes essential at every step of the book journey. Here's how:

- **Publishing.** Agents and publishers want to know *exactly* who your reader is. A fuzzy audience makes for a weak query.
- **Production.** Cover design, title, even font choice should resonate with your specific reader, not the whole world.
- **Marketing.** Doesn't matter if you're on a podcast interview or writing a LinkedIn post, you need to know where your reader spends their time so you can meet them there.

So, who is your book really for?

Exercise: Reader Persona Builder

1. Imagine your ideal reader as one person. Give them a name, age, job, and a bit of backstory. Draw them out if you want. Have fun with it!
2. Write down what they're struggling with right now. This should be the very problem your book will help solve.
3. Ask what they hope to feel after reading this book. Inspired? Equipped? Relieved? Understood?
4. Bonus: jot down where this reader hangs out (LinkedIn, conferences, parenting groups, podcasts). That's where you'll later market your book.

I promise you this:

If you can picture your reader clearly enough to imagine them sitting across from you at a coffee shop, you'll know exactly what to write and how to write it.

The Ghost's Notes

Your ideal reader isn't always obvious. I could have chosen to write this book for other entrepreneurs who want to build independent publishing houses. It would make sense, as that's part of what I do.

So, in order to decide how to move forward, I returned to my WHY.

While it could be cool, eventually, to help other businesses grow, for now my focus is on my authors.

If you read between the lines, much of this advice could still be useful to new publishers. But, the language I use and the relationship I'm building in these pages isn't precisely for them... it's for you. Do you see the difference?

Who knows? Maybe I'll make a second edition of this book geared towards the publishing community. But for now, I'm all in on you.

From WHY to WHAT

So now you've got clarity on your WHY, and your WHO. That's no small feat. Many aspiring authors skip this step entirely. Which explains why their half-finished manuscripts gather dust in a drawer.

So, take a second to give yourself a little pat on the back!

"But Adina," you're probably thinking. "When do we get to the actual writing?!"

Patience, young grasshopper. There will be plenty of time to get pen to paper.

For now, the foundational work of dismantling your faulty beliefs, uncovering your anchor, and naming your reader is reason enough to celebrate.

But, before we get too excited, there's still one big question standing in your way.

Now that you know *why* you're writing, what exactly are you going to write?

That's what we'll tackle next with your **Book Blueprint**.

Building your WHAT is the structure that will make sure you finish.

Even if you somehow snuck past the WHY and the WHO, you can't possibly skip this part.

Ready to set your compass? Let's go.

Your WHAT

> To produce a mighty book, you must choose a mighty theme.
>
> — Herman Melville

Getting Clear on What You're Really Trying to Say

Okay, it's all good and well that you know *why* you want to write a book… But what the heck are you actually going to write about?

For most first-time authors, *this* is the hardest question to answer. You likely have a jumble of stories, lessons, and opinions floating around, but you can't quite tell which one's worth a whole book, or how to tie them all together.

You're not alone. In fact, every single author I've worked with has said some version of this sentence at the start of our journey:

"I know I have a book in me… I just don't know what it's about yet."

This section is how we figure that out.

We're going to cut through the noise and get to the *core message* of your book. This is the one thing you want to say so clearly that readers can repeat it back to you in one sentence. Your book's elevator pitch, so to speak.

By the end of this section, you'll:

- Build your WHAT statement
- Do the Content Dump
- Find your through-line
- Test whether your idea is truly book-worthy
- Be able to summarize your book in one clear, confident sentence
- Feel grounded in your message before you even write your first word

Sounds like a lot, I know. Don't worry, I'm right here with you. We'll take it step by step.

And, I promise that once you find your *what*, everything else—structure, outline, and even marketing—gets easier.

I'm excited. Are you excited?!

The Fog Before the Framework

Every book starts in a kind of fog. You know you have something important to say, you're just not quite sure what that is yet. It's like walking through mist—you can see shapes in front of you, but no clear outlines.

I've seen this with almost every author I've worked with. They sit across from me on our first call, eyes wide, talking about five ideas at once. *"It's kind of about leadership,"* they'll say. *"But also resilience. And parenting. And maybe also… the importance of empathy?"*

The fog isn't something to shy away from. This uncertainty is a key element of the discovery mode you are now in.

When we first notice the fog, our instinct is to clear it. We wave our hands around, desperate to see better. But it doesn't work that way. Only when the conditions change do the outlines begin to reveal themselves.

If you try to force clarity too soon, you risk latching onto an idea that's *fine* but not *defined*. You'll know the difference when you see it.

So don't rush this part. It takes a little time for the image in front of you to develop from a blur, to a shape, and then finally something you can recognize.

That picture is your compass. This upcoming section is all about setting it.

Setting Your Compass

Open up a compass and what you'll see is simple: a magnetized needle balanced on a pivot so it can spin freely. That needle is constantly pulled into alignment with the Earth's magnetic field, always pointing to magnetic north.

Explorers have relied on compasses for centuries because of the constant point of reference it offers. No matter how lost you feel in the details, you can orient yourself by checking where north is.

The Ghost's Notes

Unfortunately, directions have always been my Achilles' heel. (If it weren't for Google Maps, I'd still be circling my own neighborhood.) But when it comes to your book, I can help you find your way.

Your book needs a single orienting point, too. And that point is your **WHAT statement.**

Your WHAT is the sentence that defines your book at a glance. It doesn't need to be clever or market-ready. It just needs to keep you oriented when you're knee-deep in messy drafts, wondering if a story belongs, or second-guessing your direction.

Some examples of strong WHAT statements:

"This is a book about how leaders can build cultures that keep people."

"This is a book about redefining resilience for entrepreneurs who are tired of hustle culture."

"This is a book about finding belonging as an immigrant in North America."

See how clear those are? They distinctly define what they're talking about and the transformation their reader can expect from reading the book.

Once you set your compass, every decision you make—from what stories to include, what arguments to cut, even what to title your book—can be checked against it. If it doesn't align with your WHAT, it doesn't belong.

Exercise: The Compass Statement

Write one sentence that starts with: *"This is a book about..."*

Try and determine what you'll cover, and what will change for the reader after reading your book.

Keep it short, clear, and specific. Don't try to be clever just yet.

Just like a compass needle points north, your WHAT will always pull you back to the heart of your book. You'll see what I mean later on.

The Ghost's Notes

I once received a 120,000-word manuscript from a client who said her book was "about the beauty industry." It tried to cover everything from history of the field, to personal memoir, critique, advice... there was no single orienting point, no north star, no compass.

Without a compass, you drift so far off course that even an editor can't pull you back. That's not where I'd want to be, if I were you! My editors scare me enough as it is! (And yes, editors have editors. We all need 'em).

With a compass, you always know if you're on track. One client of mine, Martin, started with 40+ disconnected stories from his career. Once we nailed down his WHAT, half of those stories fell away, and suddenly his book snapped into focus. BOOM!

The Content Dump

If you've been holding your stories, lessons, or frameworks inside for years, there's probably a whole volcano of ideas bubbling under the surface. And the first stage of writing a book is to stop trying to control the eruption.

When I was working with Yuliya, one of my book coaching clients, I told her, "Right now, you're the volcano. The organization will come later, but first, we need to let the lava flow."

That clicked. She stopped censoring herself. She wrote freely, wildly, joyfully... without worrying if it made any sense.

Just like a volcano doesn't critique every spurt of lava, neither should you. There'll be plenty of time for that later, I promise.

This portion of the work is what I call the **Content Dump**. It's the stage where you empty everything that's been sitting in your head and heart. Don't worry about order, structure, or grammar. This is just the time to overflow.

Here's how to do it.

Exercise: The Content Dump

1. Set a timer for 45 minutes. You might find the first few minutes are slow... and then suddenly the lava starts pouring.
2. Write *everything* that comes to mind about your topic: stories, frameworks, lessons, metaphors, quotes, conversations, passing thoughts, you name it.
3. Don't edit. Just keep your fingers moving. No one is reading this but you.
4. Do this first thing in the morning with your coffee, every day for one week.
5. Stop when you start repeating yourself. That's how you'll know the volcano's empty (for now).

A few more tips while you're in the lava flow:

- Beware the curse of knowledge. You know more than you realize. What feels obvious to you might be groundbreaking for someone else. Write it down, even if you think it's not worth sharing.
- Break it down. If you're stuck, use prompts, like:
    - "What do people always ask me about this?"
    - "What mistakes have I made (or seen others make)?"
    - "What stories illustrate this idea?"
    - "If I could only teach one thing about this topic, what would it be?"
- Keep a judgment-free zone. Editing comes later. This stage is just the release.

By the end of your Content Dump week, you'll have pages upon pages of raw material. This is your own molten foundation to shape into something solid.

The Ghost's Notes

If you're staring at a blank page, feeling like the volcano's run dry, well, congratulations! You're officially a writer.

When that happens, I turn to free association.

Free association started as a psychoanalytic technique in the early 1900s with Sigmund Freud. He thought that if you let your mind wander without censoring yourself, what comes out will reveal what's really hiding underneath.

Writers have been using this ever since. Virginia Woolf, for example, was famous for her stream of consciousness style. These were sentences that rolled on for pages, flowing straight from thought to thought without pausing to make it make sense.

The same principle can help you when you're feeling stuck in this phase.

Here's how to try it:

1) Set a timer for **five minutes.** Start writing anything. Yes, anything. If you get stuck, literally write, *"I don't know what to say right now…"* until the next thought comes.
2) Keep going until the timer goes off.
3) Then stop and read it back.

You'll be surprised by what comes out. It could be memories you didn't realize mattered, turns of phrase, insights… it could also be a whole lot of gobbledygook. That happens, too.

Free association helps you bypass the editor in your brain and get closer to what you want to say.

It's also a great journaling exercise–particularly if you write with a pen and paper. Try it!

Now we are rolling! Is it getting hot in here or is it just me?

Finding Diamonds
Among the Rocks

IF YOU'VE DONE your Content Dump properly, you likely feel a little... deflated.

You had all of this energy inside of you, and now it's... outside.

You've poured everything out–the good, the questionable, all of it.

So what happens next?

First of all, take a little break. Make yourself a nice little treat and turn off your brain with some reality TV for a while.

Then, when you're ready, it's time to look at your content dump with fresh eyes. You've erupted all your stories, lessons, and ideas onto the page. Now, we dig through the rubble and start seeing what's there.

As you begin to read through your words, you'll likely notice that certain ideas start repeating themselves. Certain stories make you pause. Some lessons feel a little *louder* than others.

This is what you need to pay attention to now.

If you have no idea what I'm talking about, let me share a few examples to make it clearer.

Let's say you're a seasoned entrepreneur with thirty years of experience. You did your content dump, and it's made up of a mix of funny stories from your early start-up days, reflections on your failures, rants about the mistakes you see other founders make, and some notes on money management in your business. At first glance, these notes feel like they're all over the place. But as you start reading through, you begin to notice:

You keep coming back to this idea of courage in early-stage entrepreneurs.

You also talk a lot about building trust with stakeholders, and what happens when that goes wrong.

And there's a persistent commentary about making decisions as a leader based on your values.

When you highlight or group those sections, you begin to realize that maybe this isn't just a random collection of stories. This could be a book about *courageous leadership built on trust and personal values.*

Those three ideas become the skeleton of your book. *Magic!*

Now you can start putting those stories into buckets. Let's say you have your "Courage" bucket, your "Trust" bucket, and your "Personal Values" bucket. Each bucket will eventually become a theme you can shape segments around.

Now let's take someone writing a memoir.

Your content dump might be filled with fragments of your old journal entries, foggy memories from childhood, snippets of dialogue you remember, and some images you just can't get out of your mind.

It might feel like a scrapbook exploded on the page. But as you start reading through, you notice that, across many of these pieces, a few things come back again and again.

There's this recurring tension between your feelings of belonging and displacement.

The bits of dialogue you shared always point to some kind of decision-making moment in your life.

Throughout all of the content pieces, there's this undercurrent of a minor feeling of identity crisis.

Those themes start whispering your story back to you. Maybe, you wonder, my book might be about finding home within yourself.

Good, good. Now you're thinking like a writer.

You'd take all those fragments and start placing them into three loose piles: *Belonging, Decision-Making, Identity.*

Then, you can take each piece of content and categorize them according to where you think they belong. Don't worry if some pieces blur between categories. Overlap is a good sign. Life is messy, so is writing.

And, if some of your content doesn't fit neatly into one of your buckets, no problem either. This is an indicator that there's yet more to your story. See if you can collect those outsider pieces and name them as a new category of their own.

Remember that, at this point, you're not signing any kind of contract stating what your book is or is not. Right now, you're simply learning what your book wants to be.

The Ghost's Notes

If this through-line doesn't magically appear, that is so completely okay. There is no magic formula for you to come to a moment of clarity. For some, it'll emerge faster than others.

Take my niece, for example. Currently, she's putting all her effort into trying to crawl. Other near-one-year-olds are pit-pattering their way around their houses, while she's desperately gliding along the smooth wooden floors. Does this mean she won't learn to crawl? No, of course not! It will come to her in time. So will your through-line.

If you're feeling stressed right now, I understand that. You want to know what your book is. You want that clarity. That makes sense. Us humans aren't huge fans of uncertainty.

I hate to say it, but right now, I'm going to need you to trust the process. Give yourself over to the uncertainty, the hole in your tummy kind of feeling. In time, this will pass, and you'll be crystal clear on your vision.

For now, though, all we need to do is some sorting.

Ready to give it a shot?

Exercise: The Bucket Sort

1. Print your content dump (yes, physically. Trust me).
2. Grab a stack of colored sticky notes or highlighters.
3. Read through everything and start marking patterns you see:

    - Recurring themes or lessons
    - Stories that feel similar or connected
    - Emotions that come up again and again

4. Start naming those categories. These are your "buckets."
5. Create a fresh document with one heading per bucket and copy and paste your relevant notes underneath each one.

By the end, you'll have a sort of proto-outline. This is not a book yet, but the bones of one.

From Themes to Thesis

But how do these buckets turn into a book?

Good question. I like the way you think. Let me tell you. Or rather, let me show you.

Steve Jobs said that "you can't connect the dots looking forward; you can only connect them looking backwards."

This was certainly true for my career. From interviewing over 100 young professionals to hosting a nightly talk show during COVID, starting a podcast in a fishing village in Ghana to spending three years as a podcast producer learning from executives across every business function... every experience was preparing me for the business I am now building. I certainly didn't know it at the time, though.

Same here, for you.

Your ideas are out, your buckets are sorted. Now it's time to connect some dots.

This is where you take all that raw material and distill it into a single unifying message, or your book's thesis statement.

We want one clear sentence that answers the question: "What is this book really about?"

This sentence becomes your north star for everything that follows. It's the beating heart of your book.

Exercise: The Message Map

You'll need:

- A blank page (or digital doc)
- Your bucketed content from the previous exercise
- A few colored markers or highlighters (if you're visual like me)

Step 1: Label Your Buckets

At the top of your page, write down the names of your three to five main themes. (If you have more, don't worry, write 'em all.)

Step 2: Find the Common Denominator

For each pair of themes, ask yourself:

- What do all these themes have in common?
- What bigger idea do they point toward?
- What problem are they all trying to solve?

You might start to see some relationships between your buckets.

Step 3: Circle the Common Thread

Look for one idea or phrase that seems to keep popping up in your answers. That's your *core thread*. It's usually something conceptual like trust, identity, resilience, freedom, belonging, courage, for example.

Step 4: Fill in the Sentence

Now, complete this simple sentence: "This is a book about [core idea], told through the lens of [your unique perspective or experience]."

Examples:

- *This is a book about belonging, told through the lens of a kid who built a business halfway around the world.*
- *This is a book about resilience, told through the lens of a founder who rebuilt her company after burnout.*
- *This is a book about leadership, told through the lens of trust and personal values.*

Step 5: Test It

Say your sentence out loud. Does it feel true? If it feels "meh," you're not quite there yet.

If it gives you that sense of *yes, that's it*, it's time to pour yourself a glass of something delicious–you've found your core message!

Step 6: One Step Further (Optional)

If you want to take it one step further, see if you can fill out this sentence:

"This is a book about [core idea], told to [ideal reader] through the lens of [your unique perspective or experience]."

If you can do this, you are ready to rumble.

<u>The Ghost's Notes</u>
This step might take longer than you expect. Don't panic!

Sometimes clarity comes in an afternoon. Sometimes it takes a week of mulling it over while you walk the dog or fold laundry. Sometimes it takes 30 years of making mistakes.

When it lands, you'll know.

Also, this is in no way the ONLY WAY to map out your why and what. There are so many ways to get from Point A to Point B. The only thing I'll stress is the importance of knowing the answers to this before you get cracking.

Lastly, I would love to hear how you identified your WHY and WHAT, your way. In all honesty, no two of my clients get there the same way.

We are so close! I can taste it!

The Idea Audit
How to Know If It's Book-Worthy

WHILE I BELIEVE everyone has a story worth sharing, not every story is quite ready to become a book.

Sometimes, the best gift you can give your idea is a little reality check. I'm not saying crush it to smithereens, but let's smooth it into marble.

Here are some ways we can stress-test the ideas you've come up with in the last section.

<u>The Ghost's Notes</u>
If your idea doesn't pass these tests, but you still feel compelled to write, please do. I am in no way prescribing what a book must look like. This is what I've learned makes for a robust and comprehensive reading experience in the current landscape, but by all means—prove me wrong.

Really, what matters to me is that you care enough to have made it this far and that you are so committed to writing. That is the most important thing. You are who I am writing for.

1. The Time Test

Will it still matter in five years?

If your topic depends on current trends, try to determine if it connects to a deeper human truth underneath them.

For example, if you're writing about AI trends, how can you connect those with the timeless concept of human creativity versus machine precision, or progress versus purpose?

2. The Depth Test

Can it hold 50,000+ words?

There are books that make me think: this could have been a blog post. If your idea can't be explored through multiple stories, questions, or frameworks, it might not have enough depth for a book yet.

Ask yourself: If I had to teach this idea, could I fill a semester?

If not, maybe you start smaller, and then build from there. Some of the best books started out as newsletters!

3. The Audience Test

Who actually needs this?

Remember, if your answer is "everyone," it's no one. We covered this in the WHY section.

Get specific here. Ironically, the sharper your focus, the wider your reach.

4. The Transformation Test

What changes for the reader?

What problem does this book solve? How will readers feel or act differently by the end?

You want to offer something to leave the reader with beyond just another number on their Goodreads list.

5. The Energy Test

Does it light you up?

You're going to spend months (or years) on this idea. If it doesn't excite you enough to keep coming back when it gets hard, it's not the one.

Ask yourself: Would I still write this if no one read it but me?

6. The Author Test

Look at the work you've done so far, and ask: why am I the right person to write this book?

Having a good answer here will quell any of those faulty beliefs and moments of impostor syndrome that might come crawling back in.

So, what did your thesis score?

If you passed at least four of the six tests, congratulations! You're ready to move on.

If not, don't panic. Revisit your buckets, your message, and your why. The idea might just need a different angle, or a bit more percolating. Another cup of coffee, anyone?

Every question you answer here is getting you closer to the book you're meant to write.

From Your WHAT to Your HOW

BUT ADINA, I've had enough of all the thinking. I want to write!

I know, I know. We are so close. I promise.

But before we write to our heart's content, we need to do one more thing. We need to shape how we're going to write what we're going to write.

This next section will help turn your book into an organized blueprint with signposts and strategy.

This is how you get to the finish line.

In this upcoming section, we'll cover:

- How to choose the natural pathway or shape of your book
- How to turn your themes and stories into a flexible Book Blueprint
- How to test that Blueprint before writing a single word

So grab a notebook. We're stepping out of the fog and into formation.

Your Book Blueprint

— Abraham Lincoln

You wouldn't start building a house without a floor plan. So why do so many authors try to write a book without a blueprint?

That's like wandering into Home Depot, buying random bits of lumber, and hoping it magically turns into a dream house.

It doesn't work. Well, I mean, you'll end up with something. But it probably won't be pretty. Or functional.

Your Book Blueprint is the tool that keeps you grounded when the writing gets messy, when you lose steam, or when you start second-guessing your vision.

Your Blueprint is NOT a Table of Contents, an outline, or a commitment to a final structure.

Your Blueprint is a living document and guided map.

By the end of this section, you'll know how to:

- Choose your pathway (memoir, how-to, hybrid, etc.)
- Identify the core elements of your book (stories, proof, tactics)
- Build your Blueprint with confidence
- Test your Blueprint with readers and Future You

This is what separates half-finished drafts from books that actually make it to print.

Ready to sharpen your axe? Right this way!

<u>The Ghost's Notes</u>

The Book Blueprint exercise might be my favorite part of working with a new author. This is basically a live version of the WHY, the WHAT, and the HOW (what you're about to read).

At the end, the author ends up with a blueprint of what their book can look like, including title options, a back cover summary, and—crucially—a detailed Table of Contents and a Book Map.

For many of my authors, this is when it starts to feel real.

One first-time author wanted to write a book about motherhood. We decided to interweave her stories with those of her mother's, writing a book that touched on generational, cultural and geographical differences of motherhood. When she saw her Blueprint, she cried.

That's what I call a job well done!

Choosing Your Pathway
What Shape Will Your Book Take?

So, you've exhaled (the content dump), inhaled (found your themes), and now you're probably wondering: What happens next?

It's time to choose what shape your book will take!

Aren't books typically rectangular?

Yes, yes, smart aleck. They are. But that's not the kind of shape I'm talking about.

The shape your book takes depends on what you're trying to say, who you're trying to say it to, and how you naturally think.

Let's walk through some of the most common shapes, and then I'll show you what I recommend for a first-timer.

Note: This is by NO MEANS a comprehensive list of all the kinds of nonfiction books you can write. Not even close. And, as I'm sure you've already guessed, your book can be more than one of these.

Pathway One: The Memoir

Memoir is one of the most beloved forms of nonfiction. But "memoir" isn't just one shape. Within this pathway, there are two primary structures you can choose from:

1. The Chronological Memoir
2. The Braided Memoir

Let's walk through each one so you can decide which fits your story best.

1. The Chronological Memoir

A chronological memoir follows your life (or a specific period of it) in order: the beginning, the middle, and the transformation that follows.

Think *Becoming* by Michelle Obama, or *When Breath Becomes Air* by Paul Kalanithi.

The beauty of this pathway is that it already has a built-in spine of time. You don't have to invent a structure from scratch.

But only a rookie would confuse *simple* with *easy*!

Contrary to what many people think, a memoir is not a chronological list of everything that's ever happened to you. (That's called a diary. And no one's reading 80,000 words on what you had for lunch in 1997.)

Writing a memoir still means making choices. What will you focus on? What will you leave out?

Who This Pathway Is For

You should consider writing a chronological memoir if:

- You've experienced a clear *before and after* in your life. Was there a defining experience or challenge that changed your perspective?
- You process things best through reflection and storytelling.
- You're writing to understand something about yourself as much as to teach others.

Pros

- The timeline keeps you grounded during the writing, since you always know what comes next.
- Writing chronologically helps you make sense of your own experiences.
- The emotional arc of struggle → growth → resolution resonates universally.

Cons

- You may feel the temptation to include everything, but just because it happened doesn't mean it belongs.
- There runs a small risk of self-indulgence. You'll need to remember that.
- The pacing might feel a little slow, so you'll need to learn how to zoom in and out.

Remember that a memoir doesn't just log what happened to you. In fact, it shouldn't even really be about you at all. It usually ends up being about what the events or experiences meant. And, in telling your story, you're opening a window for your readers to find pieces of themselves in it.

But what if your story doesn't fit neatly into a straight line? Enter "The Braided Memoir."

2. The Braided Memoir

If the chronological memoir is a straight road, the braided memoir is more like weaving threads.

Maybe you alternate between past and present, or braid together your personal story and a bigger social commentary. Maybe you explore two lives, two timelines, or two versions of yourself in conversation.

Examples of this are *Untamed* by Glennon Doyle or *Greenlights* by Matthew McConaughey. These are part story, part reflection, part meaning-making. They take you in and out of different moments in time.

A Word of Caution

I love this structure. When done well, it is elegant and rich. But it can also get confusing fast.

In the last section I mentioned my client's book about motherhood. That followed the braided structure, following her experience of raising children in North America braided with her mother's experience raising children in East Africa.

The contrast made sense here because the two storylines spoke *to* each other. They revealed the tension and tenderness between tradition and reinvention, duty and freedom, home and identity.

But if we had added a third thread—say, her grandmother's story, or a timeline about her career—the whole thing might have collapsed under its own complexity.

You need a pretty clear vision and a good reason to choose this format.

Who This Pathway Is For

You should consider a braided memoir if:

- You have two or more stories that illuminate each other.
- You think in parallels, and easily see patterns between events, people, or places.
- You're drawn to reflection as much as storytelling.

If your story lives in the *and* rather than the *then,* this might be your pathway.

Pros

- Braiding adds richness and perspective that a single thread can't quite achieve.
- You can move between tones without feeling disjointed.
- There's room to experiment with pacing, tone, and structure.

Cons

- Without clear transitions, readers can get lost.
- You'll need a strong outline to keep it all in line.
- This will likely be slower to write, since you're essentially writing two (or more) books at once and weaving them together.

If you think you might be interested in this pathway, start by writing a one-sentence summary of what each thread *is* and why it belongs.

Then, ask yourself: "When these stories sit side by side, what truth do they reveal that one story alone couldn't?"

If you can answer that, it probably makes sense for you to use this flow.

But maybe you think in moments...

Pathway Two: The Anthology, Essay, Letter & Interview Book

This is the "collection" family. Each piece stands on its own, but together, they form a chorus.

This is often how I write–in short bursts of exhilaration or desperation. Sometimes a story, sometimes a reflection, sometimes a conversation.

The through-line is usually not a single plot but the rhythm of how I think. A lot of the time it doesn't make much sense to anyone but me, but that's also kind of why I like it!

Who This Pathway Is For

You should consider this pathway if:

- You think in fragments rather than one continuous narrative.
- You love exploring ideas from different angles instead of telling a single story start to finish.
- You want your readers to be able to dip in and out of your book at their leisure.

Pros

- You can play with tone, structure, and length without worrying about a single arc.
- This is great for repurposing content–sections can live as articles, newsletters, or podcast episodes before becoming a book.
- Readers can engage with one piece at a time and still feel the whole.

Cons

- Without a strong voice or theme, it can feel scattered and disconnected.
- People like "one clear promise." Collections are often harder to pitch and market.

- When you explore similar ideas from multiple angles, you have to make sure you're not just repeating yourself.

In an anthology or collection, you are the gravitational pull holding all the pieces together. That means that your voice is what people are reading for.

When I worked in podcasting, I interviewed hundreds of executives—conversations full of insights I *should* have written down. If I had, I would have had the beginnings of an incredible interview book—each voice distinct, but all orbiting around the question: *How do people lead and live well?*

That's what this format does so beautifully. It lets you hold up many mirrors and see the same light reflected differently each time.

Pathway Three: The How-To & Field Guide

This one's for my business minds, my educators, and my consultants. These are the thinkers and doers who've built something that *works* and want to teach it in a way people can actually use.

This is for you if you've developed a process, a system, a philosophy, or even just a way of doing things that makes life or work easier.

There are two common ways to use this pathway:

- **The How-To Book**: this offers your unique roadmap that lays out your steps, pillars, or principles.
- **The Playbook / Field Guide**: this is the hands-on workbook that gets your reader moving.

You can do one or blend both. Think *Atomic Habits* (James Clear), *Start With Why* (Simon Sinek), *The Artist's Way* (Julia Cameron), or... *this book you're reading right now.*

In taking this path, you're less the hero of the story, and more of the guide.

Who This Pathway Is For

You should consider a How-To or Field-Guide book if:

- You've developed a proven system or method that gets consistent results.
- You love coaching or simplifying complex things for others.
- You catch yourself repeating the same advice in every meeting.

Pros

- Readers love a good structure.
- When someone uses your framework successfully, they become your best marketing.
- These books translate perfectly into courses and speaking engagements.

Cons

- Without stories or voice, your readers might find themselves dozing off.
- Proof is key here. You have to show that your method works in practice.
- Beware over-explaining! Once the reader "gets it," they don't want to hear it again and again and again.

Probably the most important thing to remember here is that people don't buy books because they have problems, but because they want *solutions.* The more tangible you can make your advice, the better it will land.

Now, let's move from the heart to the head for my data-loving, dot-connecting writers.

Pathway Four: The Research or Case Study Book

If you love data, stories, and evidence, this might be your lane.

You're likely the kind of person who starts sentences with, *"I read this fascinating study…"* or who has an entire Notes app folder of screenshots titled "Future Book Material."

Think *Outliers* by Malcolm Gladwell, or *Thinking, Fast and Slow* by Daniel Kahneman.

In a research or case study book, you're building an argument that is backed up by stories, data, and examples that prove your point.

Who This Pathway Is For

You should consider a research or case study book if:

- You enjoy connecting patterns across industries or disciplines.
- You have access to interesting data, studies, or stories from your field.
- You love taking complex ideas and making them make sense to anyone.

Pros

- Research-based books build instant trust with readers.
- Ideas grounded in evidence tend to age well.
- A good argument draws in professionals, students, and general readers alike.

Cons

- Gathering, verifying, and organizing research takes longer than most people think.
- Too much data and not enough story can make readers tune out.
- It's easy to get stuck endlessly researching and never writing.

Once again, this is not a comprehensive list. Choose what feels right for you.

Don't Panic!

If this is your first book, you don't need to know how to write all of these. You just need to choose a structure that gives you something that helps you move forward without overcomplicating it.

Likely one or two of these jumped out at you. Don't overthink it, just flow with it. Even though you may start on one path, it's possible you hang a left at some point, too. This is all part of the process.

So, now that you've chosen your pathway, let's build your Blueprint.

Building Your Blueprint

That last section was a lot to take in.

Let's stop for a second and recap what we've accomplished so far.

At this point in your book journey, you've overcome your limiting beliefs, identified your WHY and your WHAT, and are now in the weeds of figuring out the HOW.

If you still feel shaky on any of these fronts, that is okay. Take a step back, re-read a chapter, and come to this step when you're ready.

Before we begin, a quick bridge from the last section.

You chose the *shape* of your book. Chronological memoir. Field guide. Essay collection. That choice should guide how you build your Blueprint.

I want you to think of your Blueprint as a reference for your future self. It's not a marketing tool or a promise to a publisher. You want this to be a place of calm and clarity when you're knee-deep in a messy draft.

A great Blueprint will juggle:

- The big themes
- The supporting stories or lessons
- And the connective tissue that keeps it all flowing

It might be tempting to play with clever title options and poetic descriptions when you're filling it in, but I urge you to stick to clarity. Remember, you're not writing for readers yet. This internal Blueprint is just for you. That is, it is for Future You. And Future You will be tired, second-guessing, and probably eating trail mix for dinner, so better we make this simple.

A Quick Note Before We Begin: Don't Think in Chapters Yet

I don't recommend thinking in "chapters" at this stage. Chapters come with this sense of finality and fixedness. We're nowhere near that yet. We'll arrange, rearrange, cut, copy, paste, so we don't want to be bound by the feeling that a chapter needs to be what it is.

Right now, I suggest you think of your work in *themes*. These are loose groupings of ideas or stories that feel like they belong together. With a theme, you have full permission to experiment, move pieces around, and see how your material connects without feeling like you're making permanent decisions.

When you eventually start shaping your manuscript, some of these themes will become chapters, others might merge, and a few might disappear altogether.

This is all part of the process. Your Blueprint is NOT carved in stone.

Okay, let's begin. Deep breath.

Step 1: Write Out Your Themes

Start by opening a fresh document or page for each theme. Write the theme name at the top.

Let's say your themes are:

Courage

Belonging

Trust

You'd write those out just like that.

Step 2: Break Each Theme Down Into Stories

Then, list out everything that connects to that theme: scenes, stories, or lessons that illustrate it. You actually should have already completed this in the Finding Diamonds section. In case you thought you could sneak by without completing it, now's your second chance.

Here's an example:

Theme: Courage

- When I turned down the promotion
- Speaking up in a meeting even though I was shaking
- When I couldn't get up to go to work that Monday
- The decision-making framework I started following
- My client who took a leap using my framework

Now do the same for the other themes you've identified.

By the time you're done, you'll probably have 8-12 total stories or scenes per theme.

Each of these will eventually grow into one or more chapters.

Step 3: Write 1-2 Sentences of Story Details

For each story on your list, write a short description of what actually happens in it.

Ask yourself, in plain language:

- What is the moment?

- Who was involved?
- What happened?

Your story details might look something like this:

- I turned down a promotion I thought I was supposed to want and spent the subway ride home wondering if I'd just ruined my career.
- I spoke up in a board meeting even though my voice was shaking the whole time.
- My body shut down one morning and I fainted in my kitchen after months of ignoring stress signals.
- I walked through the four steps I now use when I need to make a big decision.
- A client told me she finally took the leap she'd been avoiding, even though she still felt terrified.

Step 4: Write a One-Line Lesson for Each Story

Now, write one sentence that starts with: "In this segment, the reader will…"

For example, Your Courage section could look something like this:

Turning down the promotion

In this story, the reader will see how chasing external validation can steer you away from your own path.

Speaking up in the boardroom

In this story, the reader will understand what everyday courage looks like in practice.

The day my body said enough

In this story, the reader will witness what happens when internal misalignment becomes impossible to ignore.

Using my decision-making framework

In this story, the reader will learn a practical way to navigate uncertainty.

My client who jumped before she felt ready

In this story, the reader will see how imperfect action often leads to the biggest breakthroughs.

These short descriptions will remind you exactly why you're including this story.

Now, we do this for every story in every theme.

Eventually, you'll end up with something like this for every theme:

Story Name: Turning Down the Promotion

I turned down a promotion everyone expected me to take and immediately panicked that I'd ruined my career. I kept asking myself why I said no when saying yes would have been so much easier.

In this story, the reader will... (Lesson)

See how chasing external validation can steer you away from your own path.

Story Name: Speaking Up When I Wanted to Hide

During a board meeting, my heart was pounding and my palms were sweaty, but I forced myself to speak up even though I felt completely out of my depth.

In this story, the reader will... (Lesson)

Understand what everyday courage looks like in practice.

Story Name: The Day My Body Said Enough

One morning I nearly fainted after months of ignoring exhaustion, and the doctor told me I needed to stop working immediately.

In this story, the reader will... (Lesson)

Witness what happens when internal misalignment becomes impossible to ignore.

Learning to Make Hard Decisions

I walked myself through the decision-making process I now teach others, trying to choose between two equally risky paths with no clear right answer.

In this story, the reader will... (Lesson)

Learn a practical way to navigate uncertainty.

My Client Who Jumped Before She Felt Ready

A client of mine finally launched her business even though she insisted she "wasn't ready," and it completely changed her life trajectory

In this story, the reader will... (Lesson)

See how taking imperfect action often leads to breakthroughs.

Step 5: Review for Flow

Once everything is on the page, take a step back and look at how they fit together.

- Does one idea clearly lead to the next?
- Are there emotional or logical gaps?
- Does something feel repetitive or out of place?

A few tricks to help you test your own flow:

- Print it out and read it aloud. You'll feel when something jumps out of place.
- Look for echoes. If two stories teach the same lesson, merge them or choose the stronger one.

When you find an order that *feels right*, trust that sensation. It's usually your story telling you where it wants to go.

Make sense? Yeah?

Prove it. It's your turn!

Exercise: Your Blueprint Draft

- List your themes.
- Under each theme, list 8-12 stories.
- Add a few details you want to include in the stories.
- Write a one-sentence "In this section, the reader will…"
- Review for alignment with your WHY and WHAT. Rearrange if needed. You will likely do this multiple times during the writing process.

Pro Tip:
When you get stuck, ask yourself:

- What theme does this story belong to?
- What lesson does it teach?

That's how you keep your writing aligned with your book's purpose.

Now, upload or print your first Blueprint draft. Keep it somewhere visible. You'll need it when you start writing.

The Ghost's Notes
The clearer you are now about what you want to say, the easier writing will be later. This exercise means you will never face a totally blank page.

Yes, this stage can feel a little torturous. I know the feeling all too well.

But I promise that Future You will thank you.

In fact, this applies to more than just books. It's a pretty good life philosophy too… Maybe I should forget about this book coaching thing and be a life coach!

Nope. My Blueprint that helped me build this book won't let me digress like that. Back to regularly scheduled programming, folks.

An aside: I only thought about adding The Ghost's Notes after I was three quarters done writing this book. That proves the point. Your Blueprint will evolve. But you need something on the page first. That is the only way to move forward.

Testing Your Blueprint

Wait a second. Hold on. Everybody stop.

Is this map even taking you where you want to go?

Before you dive into writing, you want to make sure your Blueprint aligns with two essential things: **Your WHY** and **your READER**.

Why are we going backwards?

Well, here's what often happens:

Somewhere between the idea and the Blueprint, writers start to drift. You'll find yourself thinking, "Ooh, maybe I should add a section on..." or "What if I turned this into a totally different book?"

That's normal. But if we give in to each of our whims and fantasies, we'll never get anything done.

Revisit Your WHY

Remember the reason you started this whole thing in the first place? This is where you make sure your Blueprint still reflects it.

Ask yourself:

- Does this Blueprint still serve the reason I wanted to write this book in the first place?
- Does every major theme connect, in some way, to that deeper reason I care about this topic?

If your WHY was to help other women navigate career reinvention, ask yourself if that thread shows up in every segment.

If your WHY was to capture your father's stories before they fade, are those stories still central, or did they get lost in side tangents about business strategy?

You might find that some sections belong in *your next* book. Better to uncover that now.

Revisit Your WHAT Statement

Pull out your compass statement from earlier. This is that single sentence that starts with "This is a book about..."

Now read through your Blueprint, slowly, and ask:

- Does each story clearly connect back to that main point?
- Are there any ideas that feel like they belong to a different book entirely?
- If someone read my Blueprint alone, would they immediately understand what this book is *about*?

Do the Reader Walkthrough

Imagine your *ideal reader* (the one you defined earlier). Now, walk through your Blueprint *as if you're them* and ask:

- What am I learning here?
- What am I feeling?
- What's motivating me to keep reading?

This is likely where you'll start to see some important gaps... maybe you jump too quickly from problem to solution, or maybe the emotional arc is missing a beat. You might realize: "Oh, this story belongs way earlier."

That's a good sign. It means you're seeing your book from the outside now.

What to Do If Your Blueprint Doesn't Feel Right (Yet)

So, you've done all the work. You have your clusters, your segments, your one-liners and your key stories and ideas.

You're looking at your beautiful Blueprint, thinking:

"Hmm. Something's... off."

First of all, *good*. That means you're paying attention.

Every single author hits this point. It's the moment of panic where you start wondering: Did I pick the right angle? Is this even the book I wanted to write? Does this mean I have to start over completely?

Now, before you spiral, try this:

- **Step away for a day or two.** Fresh eyes are magic.
- **Ask one trusted reader:** "Does this feel coherent to you?"
- **Circle the parts that *do* feel right.**
- **Revisit your WHY and your compass.** Nine times out of ten, that's where the drift happened.

Sometimes your first Blueprint is just a *draft* of your real book idea.

Stay calm. You're not lost. You're just in the middle of finding your true north.

What Comes Next

You've done it! You've built your foundation.

You've faced the faulty beliefs, defined your why, mapped your reader, set your compass, dumped your content, found your themes, shaped your stories, and tested your Blueprint against your purpose.

That's no small thing. Or things.

Most people stay stuck in the "I should write a book one day" phase forever. You're already miles ahead because you've turned that idea into a plan.

Okay, enough with the thinking and clarifying and organizing.

Now we are ready to roll up our sleeves and get writing!

This next part is where you build your writing muscle. Showing up, even when you're not "inspired," finding a writing rhythm that fits into your life, and keeping your motivation alive.

Writing & Accountability

For a long time, I thought "writer" was a title you had to earn. Like there was a secret committee somewhere handing out badges. But I've been writing for as long as I can remember, and no one ever came knocking on my door.

At some point, I realized that being a writer isn't something you wait to be told you are. It's something you decide to be. You just need to start putting words on the page, consistently enough that your ideas begin to take shape.

You need to let yourself write.

There's no wrong way to do it. Heck, hold the pen in between your toes! If what comes out is a string of words—who's to say that doesn't count?!

The real obstacle in writing a book is the consistent dedication to getting it done.

This part of the book is about building that structure. Because once you've set your compass and mapped your ideas, the only thing standing between you and a finished book is *the work itself.*

Here's a hot take of mine: I don't believe in writer's block. Think about people who are paid to write. Journalists. Copywriters. Screenwriters. They can't just take a day off because "inspiration isn't hitting." They show up anyway. This is not because they're magical creatures immune to creative struggle. It's because they have systems.

That's the thing most first-time authors don't realize: there's no point waiting for the muse to visit. Instead, you need to build the right structures so you can show up and do the work, even when you don't feel like it.

This section of the book will help you with:

- Setting realistic writing goals
- Building a writing rhythm
- Drafting without editing
- Staying organized
- Staying accountable
- Overcoming resistance

You don't have to wait until you feel like a writer. You just have to write.

Ready? Let's get started.

Setting Realistic Writing Goals

 I write only when inspiration strikes. Fortunately, it strikes every morning at nine o'clock sharp.

— W. Somerset Maugham

HERE'S something most people get wrong about writing a book: the secret to writing is not discipline, or talent, or divine inspiration. It actually all comes down to one thing: math.

What? Math?! The whole reason I became a writer was to get as far away from Calculus as possible. How did we end up back here?

Bear with me.

When people tell me they "don't have time" to write a book, I always think of my client Ron. I already introduced you to Ron earlier, but let's go a little deeper to understand his process.

Ron is a busy person. If he's not in meetings, he's listening to audiobooks. If he's not listening to audiobooks, he's on a sales call. If he's not on a sales call, he's giving a lecture. If he's not giving a lecture, he's taking his son to soccer practice. You get the idea.

But Ron was insistent on writing his book. How did he get it done? He decided that he'd dedicate 30 minutes a day to writing, no matter what. Just 30 minutes, each day.

Six months later, he had a complete manuscript.

"A small daily task, if it be really daily, will beat the labors of a spasmodic Hercules." - Anthony Trollope

Let's do the math.

If you write 500 words a day, five days a week, that's 2,500 words per week. In five months, that's roughly 50,000 words. This is the length of a publishable nonfiction book.

500 words a day isn't a heroic sprint. It actually amounts to just two or three pages. That could be just half an hour of focused thought, especially if you're working off of a robust outline. This is absolutely doable. But it only works if you commit to consistency over intensity.

Let's put this to the test!

Build Your Writing Goals

1. Decide how many days per week you can realistically write.
2. Pick your daily word goal (start small, like 300-500 words).
3. Multiply your weekly total by 24 weeks (6 months).
4. Voilà, you have your projected draft length.

Building a Writing Rhythm

> We are what we repeatedly do. Excellence, then, is not
> an act, but a habit.

> — Aristotle

Motivation is unreliable. It's emotional. It spikes and fades.

Rhythm, on the other hand, is reliable. It's what happens when your brain learns that *at this time, in this place, I write.*

Neuroscientists call this context-dependent memory. Your brain associates certain environments and cues with certain actions. When you build a consistent writing rhythm, you're wiring your brain to switch into creative mode automatically.

That's why you can't rely on willpower alone to write this book. Willpower is a finite resource. It depletes with every decision you make throughout the day. But systems (think scheduled writing blocks, rituals, or cues) remove decision fatigue altogether.

The Habit Loop

According to Charles Duhigg, author of *The Power of Habit*, every habit has three parts: a cue, a routine, and a reward.

A cue is the trigger that tells your brain it's time to write (e.g., morning coffee, opening your laptop, sitting at the same spot).

A routine is the act of writing itself.

And the reward is the payoff. This could be checking your word count, ticking off a box, or a second cup of coffee.

Repeat that loop often enough, and your brain starts craving the reward. Writing becomes a behavior you *want* to repeat. Anyone else hear Pavlov's dog barking?

How You Can Build Your Writing Rhythm

Choose your trigger. Something repeatable: same time, same place, same beverage or little treat.

Set a realistic time block. 15-30 minutes. Think short and consistent over long and infrequent.

Track your streak. Visible progress activates dopamine, which is your brain's "feel-good" chemical. It'll leave you wanting more of that feeling.

End on a high note. Hemingway famously said, "Stop when you still have something to say." That anticipation makes it easier to return the next day. It's like taking your kid home from the park while they're still enjoying it—not once they're face down in the sandpit with a bruised knee. You can do this by ending your writing session in the middle of a chapter, for example, so you have something to look forward to completing the next day.

So, right now, pull out your calendar and block out your writing windows for the week ahead.

Drafting Without Editing

 Write drunk, edit sober.

— Ernest Hemingway

(METAPHORICALLY, of course... though I'm not here to judge your process.)

One of the biggest mistakes I see new writers make is that they try to write and edit at the same time.

They'll get one paragraph down, then spend twenty minutes tweaking commas, rewriting sentences, or rearranging their opening line. Before they know it, an hour has passed, and they've written... forty words.

The problem here is that they're asking their brain to do two completely opposite things at once.

The Science Behind This

Your brain has two major "modes" of thinking:

1. **The Creator Mode**: this is spontaneous, intuitive, and free-flowing. This is your *default mode network*, the part of the brain active during daydreaming, storytelling, and creative ideation.
2. **The Editor Mode**: this is analytical, precise, and rule-bound. This is your *executive control network*, which lights up when you evaluate, critique, or fix problems.

The problem is that these two systems can't run efficiently at the same time. They compete for cognitive resources. When you switch between them, you interrupt your brain's natural creative flow.

Neuroscientists call this task-switching cost, and it's the reason context switching kills productivity. Every time you jump between drafting and editing, you burn mental fuel just getting your brain to refocus.

I once interviewed Dr. Art Markman, a cognitive psychologist and professor at the University of Texas at Austin, who taught me the truth about multitasking.

"People think multitasking means doing two things at once," he said, "but really it just means switching between them very quickly, and paying a cost every single time you do."

We may think we're being efficient when we fix as we go. But what we're really doing is making our brains start from scratch over and over again.

This is why so many writers feel "blocked." But they're not blocked. They're just held up by perfectionism.

A Better Way to Draft

When you sit down to write, your only job is to get words on the page. Not *perfect* words, just *existing* ones. You can't fix what isn't written.

Here's what I recommend to my clients (and what I practice myself):

1. **Separate creation from correction.** Have two distinct sessions: one for writing, and one for editing. Even if it's later that same day, label them differently so your brain knows which mode it's in.
2. **Set a "no backspace" rule for your draft sessions.** Tape a sticky note on your screen that says: *Don't touch the backspace key.* Let the ugly sentences stay. Future You will clean them up later.
3. **Use placeholders.** Stuck on a word? Write "[better word here]" and keep going. If a research detail is missing, just add "[insert data later]."
4. **Try sprint writing.** Use a timer for 25 minutes on, 5 minutes off. This time pressure forces you to outrun your inner editor.

Exercise: Daily Sprint Tracker

Each writing session, record your start time, end time, and total words written. At the bottom, write one line: *Did I stay in Creator Mode?*

No one's ever published a book they only *thought* about writing perfectly. They publish the one they actually finished.

Staying Organized

 Your mind is for having ideas, not holding them.

— David Allen

A CLIENT once came to me after losing **10,000 words** of her manuscript. Ten. Thousand. My heart still breaks when I think about it.

Her laptop had crashed, and the only copy of her work lived in a single Word document on her desktop. There was no backup, no version history, no Google Drive. Just one fragile file standing between her and heartbreak. The horror!

I wish I could say this was rare. It's not.

Writers tend to romanticize chaos. The idea of scattered notes, the "I know it's somewhere in here", the 15 open tabs… I've been here. I find myself here often, actually.

But a key thing I come back to over and over again is *organization*. This is how you respect your creativity enough to make sure it survives.

The Science of Creative Clarity

Your brain can only hold about 3-4 items in working memory at a time. Cognitive psychologists call this *cognitive load*.

When your drafts are scattered across folders, sticky notes, and 19 different Google Docs titled "Book Stuff (Final FINAL for real this time)," your brain is burning energy just trying to *find things*.

That's precious energy that could be going toward writing!

When you externalize structure through folders, naming conventions, and backups, you're freeing up cognitive space for what your brain needs to be focusing on: getting words on the page!

File System Foundations

Here's the long and short of it: You should be able to spill coffee on your laptop and still sleep at night.

How?!

You need one central cloud-synced home for your project (Google Drive, Notion, Dropbox... whatever you actually use). This is the 21st century, people! There are no excuses for your dog eating your homework anymore.

Every file should tell you exactly what it is.

Book_Title_Draft1_2026-03-01 is clear.

NEW_DRAFT_OMG_use_this_one is not.

Version Control as Creative Freedom

Another golden rule: Never overwrite your drafts.

Each new version should live as its own file, dated and labeled. The safety of knowing that that once sentence that you went back and forth on still lives in a past draft actually frees you to make changes.

If you're working in Google Docs, there's a great feature called

"Version History." (I can't tell you how many times this has saved my behind).

Your Idea Capture System

It's unreasonable to expect all your great ideas to come only when you sit down to write. Sometimes they arrive while you're washing dishes, walking the dog, or mid-shower when you're defenseless and shampoo-handed.

That's why every writer needs an **idea capture system.**

Pick one place where stray thoughts go to live. This can be your Notes app, an email thread sent to yourself, a voice memo folder, even a pocket notebook.

Then, once a week, transfer those ideas into your main structure.

Exercise: File System Setup Guide

Take 30 minutes to get your creative house in order.

1. Choose your main storage platform (Drive, Notion, Dropbox, etc.).
2. Create your folder structure and label clearly.
3. Save your latest draft as a dated version.
4. Back it up in at least one other place.
5. Set a recurring calendar reminder for a weekly backup check.

Remember: nothing kills a great idea faster than not being able to find it.

Staying Accountable

You've met Fred already. He is one of my beloved book coaching clients. He is a thoughtful man, and one who is inspired often only under duress. In the beginning of our work together, I wasn't quite sure if he'd ever get down to any actual writing. His rhythm was all over the place, his ideas scattered. For some time, I wondered if I was actually doing him any good.

Then one day, we decided to try something new.

See, Fred is a self-proclaimed "YouTube hound." Documentaries, interviews, old war footage... you name it, he watches it. He'd been slacking with his writing, so we made a pact: If he wants to turn on YouTube, he first has to sit at his desk and write for 15 minutes. If nothing comes out, that's fine. If it turns into an hour, even better.

Fred and I had accidentally stumbled into something psychologists call 'habit stacking' and 'immediate rewards.' These happen to be two of the most effective tools for maintaining accountability.

How do they work? I'll show you.

Habit Stacking

In *Atomic Habits*, James Clear popularized this concept: if you want to build a new habit, anchor it to an existing one.

"I will [new habit] after I [current habit]."

For Fred, that meant: "I will watch WWII documentaries on Youtube after I sit down to write for 15 minutes."

The existing habit = *watching YouTube*

The stacked habit = *writing first*

The writing managed to just slip into his daily routine.

Immediate Rewards

The second part of the equation is the reward. You want your brain to instantly associate the new habit with something enjoyable, so that you keep doing the new thing.

For Fred, YouTube became the reward for writing.

All of a sudden, writing became his favorite part of the day, because it unlocked his Youtube time!

As Clear puts it, "You do not rise to the level of your goals. You fall to the level of your systems."

Fred finally had a system!

Build Your Own Habit: Action/Reward Stack

1. Choose one habit you already do every single day.
2. Choose the tiniest possible writing action to stack onto it.
3. Combine them using the habit-stacking formula: "After I [existing habit], I will [tiny writing action]."
4. Add your reward.
5. Test it out for one week.

The Psychology of Accountability

Accountability works best when it's visible, immediate, and specific. Let's break those three elements down:

1. **Visible:** Track your progress somewhere you can see it. This could be a calendar, spreadsheet, or writing app. I personally love a good detailed Google Sheet. Every check triggers a dopamine hit, reinforcing the behavior.
2. **Immediate:** Don't wait until you've finished your whole book to feel proud. Reward the micro-wins. A page written, a section drafted, a messy outline clarified all count.
3. **Specific:** "Write this week" is vague. "Write 500 words on Tuesday morning before work" is concrete. Ambiguity will kill your momentum.

Find Your Kind of Accountability

Everyone's motivated differently. Some writers thrive on community, like weekly check-ins and coaching calls. Others prefer more personal systems.

Here are a few you can try:

- **Peer accountability:** find one person to exchange word counts or progress updates with each week.
- **Public accountability:** post your weekly writing intention on LinkedIn or in your newsletter.
- **Coach accountability:** schedule recurring check-ins with someone who won't let you hide from your goals (hi, remember me?).
- **Self-accountability:** set clear rules and rewards for yourself like "I can watch Netflix once I have written 500 words."

Whatever you choose, consistency is your greatest ally.

The Ghost's Notes

My friend Mike and I have been sending a weekly accountability email to each other for over a year now.

Each week, we write down our wins, our challenges, our goals, and review our goals from the week prior.

This has been a hugely motivating accountability system. It's also so rewarding to go back and read through our progress!

Overcoming Resistance

WHY IS it that I only feel the urge to work on something when the deadline is looming over me like a fire-breathing dragon?

Seriously. Give me two weeks to finish a task, and I'll find thirteen other "urgent" things to do: reorganize my Notion dashboard, alphabetize my spice rack (for me this usually starts with "Pepper" and ends with "Salt"), deep clean my email inbox from 2012. But the night before an edit needs to be sent to a client, suddenly, you can just call me Shakespeare.

If this sounds familiar, congratulations. You're human. Join the club.

The Science of Resistance

When faced with something big and uncertain (like writing a book), your brain interprets it as a threat. The fear of failure, judgment, or not being "good enough" activates your brain's amygdala, which is the same system responsible for fight, flight, or freeze responses.

And since you can't physically run away from your manuscript, your brain finds a creative loophole: it distracts you. It tells you that vacuuming the baseboards is suddenly the most urgent task in the world. (My apartment has never looked so clean.)

Dr. Tim Pychyl, a psychologist who studies procrastination, calls this **"mood repair."** When a task feels emotionally uncomfortable, we choose a different one that provides short-term relief. That's why reorganizing your notes feels productive, but really, it's just avoidance wearing a clever disguise.

How You Can Outsmart Resistance

The trick is to *anticipate* that resistance and make it irrelevant. Here's how to do that:

1. Shrink the threat.

Break your writing sessions into chunks so small your brain doesn't register them as scary.

"Write my book" = panic but "Write 200 words about this one story" = doable. This takes us all the way back to our Blueprint.

2. Externalize your commitment.

When you share your goal out loud (with your coach, writing buddy, or your neighbor), you transform a private fear into a public promise. And the brain *hates* breaking promises. This is social wiring 101. Read more on that in Dr. Robert Cialdoni's *Persuasion*. Good stuff in there.

3. Make the first 5 minutes sacred.

Research from *The Zeigarnik Effect* shows that once you start a task, your brain becomes uncomfortable leaving it unfinished. That means the hardest part is literally starting. Set a timer for five minutes and just begin. Your brain will do the rest.

4. Reward progress.

Give yourself micro-rewards (Fred would approve). Every time you overcome resistance, acknowledge the win. The reward loop helps your brain link "writing" with "positive emotion" instead of total dread. Just try not to make every reward a piece of chocolate. Been there, done that. My gut health didn't thank me.

Exercise: The Resistance Map

Draw two columns:

Column 1: Your avoidance habits

List the things you do when you're "fake working." (Mine include: mopping the floor, watering the plants, and baking oatmeal chocolate chip cookies.)

Column 2: Your replacement actions

Write what you'll do instead next time resistance hits. (e.g., "Write one messy paragraph," or "Set a five-minute timer.")

Remember this: dragons only breathe fire when you run from them. Turn toward the pages, and they tend to quiet down.

The Ghost's Notes

Sleep beckons.

Amazon Prime whispers that there's only one more episode in the season.

Will I give in?

Probably, sometimes.

But will I come back to writing? I have no other choice!

Practical Tools That Actually Get Words on the Page

OKAY, so you've got the systems. You've got the rhythm. You've even made peace with your inner procrastinator.

Now let's talk about the actual *writing*.

Here are three ways to put pen to paper:

Write by Asking (and Answering) Questions

When most writers sit down to "write Chapter 3," their brain panics. It feels too huge and abstract.

So don't write "a chapter." Write *answers*.

Turn each section into a question:

- "What story best illustrates this idea?"
- "What was I feeling in that moment?"
- "What lesson did I learn here?"
- "If someone were sitting across from me asking for advice, what would I say?"

These questions move your brain from performance mode into *conversation mode.*

When I coach my authors, I often have them "interview themselves" using a simple framework like the one below.

Exercise: Interview Yourself

1. Write down five questions you think your readers would ask you about your story or topic.
2. Answer each one conversationally, just like you're explaining it to a friend.

Now all you have to do is just answer your way through the page.

Borrow Your Speaking Voice

If you've ever given a presentation, explained your work to a colleague, or told a great story at dinner, you already know how to communicate clearly. Writing is just that, on paper.

So, when in doubt, speak it out.

Record yourself talking through a concept or story. Pretend you're explaining it to a client or student. Then transcribe it with tools like Otter, or Descript. I find ChatGPT to be great at voice-to-text.

Most of my ghostwriting clients are shocked the first time they see their own transcripts. Did I really say that? They ask. They realize they *already sound like an author.* They just needed a way to capture it.

Pro tip: the most natural and engaging writing often comes straight from spoken words that were later cleaned up for clarity.

<u>The Ghost's Notes</u>
I love talk-to-text. This is how I prep all of my LinkedIn content.

I might look like a maniac muttering to myself in public, but it saves me so much time, and is a great way for me to just reflect on my week.

Write the Too Long; Didn't Read (TL;DR) Version First

Where do I even begin?

If this thought has crossed your mind, the TL;DR version might be the method for you.

Instead of aiming to write the whole story or concept, write the shortest possible version in just two minutes. This is basically like creating a mini outline for your page. Digital writer Nicholas Cole calls this "prepping the page." You move away from that perfectionist voice inside of you and just get something down on paper.

Then, once the two minutes are up, you can go in and fill what's missing.

The Real Secret to Finishing Your Book

By now, you've built the foundation that separates writers who dream about books from writers who finish them. You have:

- A realistic plan that makes writing fit your life
- A rhythm that keeps you consistent
- Systems to stay organized and sane
- Accountability to keep you showing up
- Tools to quiet resistance and move through it
- And techniques to get the words out of your head and onto the page

If you can't tell yet, you already have everything you need to write this book. Not one day. Not "when you have time." Now.

So, what are you waiting for?

Open your document. Write the worst first sentence you can possibly think of.

And remember: you can't edit a blank page.

Editing & Refinement

Turning Your Draft Into a
Professional Manuscript

I'm not a very good writer, but I'm an excellent rewriter.

—James A. Michener

YOU DID IT! You wrote the thing. You survived the blank-page standoffs and all the scary fire-breathing resistance-dragons.

Now you've got... words. Lots of them.

Let me guess how you're feeling right now:

Probably not how you thought you'd feel. Am I right?

Finishing your first draft is exciting, yes. But it's also a little disorienting.

You might be thinking, *Okay, I've finished my manuscript. But I'm not happy with what I'm looking at. This is not what I envisioned.*

Talk about a let down. You've climbed one mountain only to look up and realize there's another one waiting.

Editing is that second mountain. Now you have to take the rough shape of your ideas and sculpt them. This is the process of discovering what you really meant to say in the midst of all of those words...

<u>The Ghost's Notes</u>
If I'm being honest, I think editing a book is harder than writing one.
Sorry to break it to you! Mordor's mountains loom ahead.

After an edit, your words will sound the way you always hoped they would.

Unfortunately, the edit is also where a lot of writers get lost.
Some over-edit until all the energy is gone. Others under-edit, afraid to touch what they've created.

Just to be clear: neither works.

But I'll show you what does!

Together, we'll learn:

- The four levels of editing (developmental, line, copy, proof) and what each one actually does.
- How to know when your draft is "good enough" to move forward.
- And how to work *with* editors, not against them, to get your book across the finish line.

The Four Levels of Editing

Some writers think their book just needs "a quick proofread." But every editor knows that's never true.

Editing has four distinct layers, each with its own purpose. Think of them as zooming in from 30,000 feet all the way down to the individual bricks. Let's break them down.

1. Developmental Editing

This is the big-picture edit. You can think of it as the *structural engineering* of your book.

A developmental editor looks at the architecture of your manuscript and asks:

- Does the structure make sense?
- Are the chapters in the right order?
- Are there missing pillars or redundant sections?
- Is there a clear through-line connecting everything?

This is where we zoom out to make sure your ideas are solid before we get into sentence-level details.

Now, if you've followed my process, you shouldn't need a developmental editor. Your ducks should all be in a row. But, if something still feels off in your book (maybe it feels a little wobbly, or unfocused) getting a bird's eye view can definitely help.

Pro Tip: Don't get too attached to your current structure. Even published authors move chapters, cut entire sections, and rewrite openings at this stage.

The Ghost's Notes

I learned the phrase "kill your darlings" when I worked in the podcast industry. No matter how much time you spent scripting that intro, sometimes, it's just gotta go.

2. Line Editing

Once the structure is solid, we can zoom in. Line editing makes your writing become *readable*.

This stage focuses on:

- The flow of ideas from one paragraph to the next
- Pacing and tone
- Word choice, rhythm, and clarity
- Strengthening your voice so it sounds consistent throughout

Example:

Before: "She was of the belief that success was dependent on hard work."

After: "She believed success came from hard work."

Line editing helps to make your prose sing.

3. Copyediting

Okay, it's time to pull out your microscope! A copyedit polishes the details:

- Grammar, punctuation, and syntax
- Consistency of terms, tense, capitalization, and formatting
- Factual accuracy (did you spell that name right? Was it 2018 or 2019?)

The Ghost's Notes
Nothing pulls a reader out of a story faster than a typo—unless that's just me? I used to underline mistakes in published books (as if the publishers could see). I always thought that'd be a genius way to get hired as an editor. Just bring in all the existing books I'd redlined to prove I could do a better job than the people they paid!

Pro Tip: A good copyedit should refine your existing style. You should still very much sound like you, just you on your best day.

4. Proofreading

Proofreading is the last pass before publication.

At this point, you're checking for surface-level errors that slipped through:

- Typos
- Missing periods
- Extra spaces
- Formatting inconsistencies

It's like running back into the house after locking the door, just to triple-check that you did, in fact, turn off the stove.

The Ghost's Notes

I used to be (okay, maybe still am) TERRIFIED of sending anything over for edit.

My stomach would clench, my fists curl. This is it, I'd think. This is where I get exposed as a fraud.

But, I am learning that my ideal editor is rigorous but kind. I want someone who will push my work, and sharpen my voice.

A good editor should make your book more you than you ever imagined.

Self-Editing Your Draft
The Three-Pass Edit

By now, it should be clear that no one writes a clean first draft. What makes great authors stand out isn't that they get it right the first time, but that they know how to get it right later.

The key is to approach your draft in three deliberate passes, each with a distinct purpose. Let's go through them one by one.

Pass One: Structure & Substance

Focus: What's working (and what isn't) at the big-picture level.

This is your "forest view." Ask yourself:

- Does each chapter serve the book's overall purpose?
- Is the order logical and emotionally satisfying?
- Does the reader always know where we are and why it matters?
- Are there sections that repeat the same point?

Mark anything that feels confusing, redundant, or out of place.

But resist the urge to fix it yet. You're mapping the terrain before you start rearranging trees.

Pro tip: I really like printing things out. A change of format helps me see the structure more objectively.

Pass Two: Style & Flow

Focus: How the writing *feels* on the page.

Once your structure makes sense, it's time to refine your sentences.

- Do your sentences vary in length and cadence?
- Are you using active voice where possible?
- Is your tone consistent with your purpose and audience?
- Are there spots where you can tighten without losing warmth?

Try reading aloud. This is the fastest way to hear what's working and what isn't.

Pro tip: If you stumble while reading, your reader will too.

Pass Three: Precision & Polish

Focus: The details that make your book feel professional.

Now you can zoom all the way into the grammar, punctuation, consistency, and formatting. This is where you catch the sneaky typos, dangling commas, and stylistic hiccups that survived the first two passes.

Ask:

- Am I consistent with headings, bullet styles, and capitalizations?
- Are names, numbers, and timelines accurate?

- Does my formatting match industry standards (margins, spacing, font)?

Pro tip: Do this stage in short bursts. And, keep a note of any unique spelling choices to make sure you're being consistent with the decisions and changes you're making.

The 24-Hour Rule

Between each pass, take at least a day off. Your brain needs time to switch from *writer* to *editor*. When you come back with some distance, you'll see things you couldn't before.

Once you've done these passes, you're ready for the next stage: collaborating with a professional editor who can elevate your manuscript even further.

But, Before You Hand It Off...

By now, you've lived with your draft long enough to know every word by heart, which also means you've probably gone *word-blind*. That's normal. Every author reaches this point.

Before you send your manuscript to a professional editor, there's one powerful step that too many writers skip: getting reader feedback from real people who represent your target audience.

This next step is how you find out how your book actually lands in the wild.

Inviting Beta Readers

Before your manuscript moves into the professional editing or design stage, it's worth putting it through the beta read.

Beta readers are volunteers who provide feedback on your manuscript from the perspective of an average reader. They are not editors, and they're not there to praise or nitpick. They're there to tell you how your book feels to read.

You want to know things like:

- Where did they skim or lose interest?
- What parts made them feel something?
- Were there moments where they wanted *more* (context, clarity, examples)?
- Did anything feel repetitive or confusing?

Who Makes a Good Beta Reader

Not your mom. Not your best friend. And definitely not anyone who's afraid to hurt your feelings.

The best beta readers are your *intended audience*. If you're writing a book on starting a business, ask other entrepreneurs. If it's a memoir, find readers who connect with your themes.

Just three readers is plenty. Any more, and you'll drown in feedback.

How to Use Beta Readers Effectively

- **Be clear about what you want.** Send them 3-5 guiding questions (e.g., "Where did you get bored?" or "What was your biggest takeaway?").
- **Give a deadline.** Two to three weeks is ideal. Any longer, and momentum fades.
- **Look for patterns.** If one person says a section drags, that's opinion. If three people do, that's data.
- **Thank them generously.** A gift card and a signed copy of the book when published goes a long way.

Where This Fits in the Process

Here's how it looks in context:

1. You finish your self-edits.
2. You send the draft to beta readers for honest feedback.
3. You make small adjustments based on their insights.
4. *Then* you hand it to your professional editor for the line or copyedit.

That's how you ensure you're not paying an editor to fix what a reader could have told you first.

Beta Reader Feedback Template

Create a simple document with the following prompts:

1. What parts of the book did you enjoy most?
2. Where did you lose interest?
3. Was there anything confusing or unclear?
4. What stuck with you after reading?
5. What's one suggestion you'd make to improve it?

This is your final tune-up before you hand it off to the professionals.

The Ghost's Notes

I have a confession. Against my own advice, I had my parents and my sister be my beta readers.

In response to the questions above, here's what my mom had to say:

What parts of the book did you enjoy most? **All**

Where did you lose interest? **Nowhere**

Was there anything confusing or unclear? **Only the Table of Contents part**

What stuck with you after reading? **I can apply this to my art!**

What's one suggestion you'd make to improve it? **It's perfect! Just fix the Table of Contents part.**

Now do you see why your mom isn't the most objective person to give you feedback?

And yes, I did fix the Table of Contents part. Thanks, Mom!

Working With Professional Editors

> To write is human, to edit is divine.
>
> — Stephen King

THERE COMES a point in every writer's journey when you've done everything you can on your own.

You've wrestled with the structure, massaged the sentences, chased down typos, and now your manuscript is whispering (or shouting), *"I need another pair of eyes."*

That's your cue to bring in a professional editor.

Why Working With an Editor Matters

You are too close to your own work to see it clearly.

An editor's job is to read your book *as a stranger would*.

A good editor is your mirror, your advocate, and your truth-teller all in one. They help you strengthen your argument, clarify your message, and preserve your voice while making it more powerful.

What to Look For in an Editor

Your editor will become your closest collaborator. Choose wisely.

Here's what I recommend looking for:

1. Alignment.

They should understand your *genre, goals, and tone.* A memoir editor isn't the same as a business book editor.

2. Communication.

Do they explain their process clearly? Offer timelines and pricing up-front? Good editing requires transparency. There should be no mysterious fees or "we'll see when we get there" agreements.

3. Respect for voice.

If an editor rewrites your sentences so much that it stops sounding like you, that's more like ventriloquism than editing.

4. Curiosity.

Editors who ask smart questions usually give smart feedback. You want someone who probes with curiosity.

How to Be a Great Editing Partner

Working with an editor is a two-way street. You, the author, must stay open and curious, and your editor needs to meet you with respect and skill.

Here's how I'd recommend making the most of that relationship:

1. Be Open, Not Defensive

No editor worth hiring is trying to "catch" you doing something wrong.

But, since we're all humans, feedback can still sting. You've poured your heart, your voice, maybe even your childhood memories onto the page and then someone comes along with the dreaded Track Changes function and starts poking at them. Ouch. It's normal to feel protective.

So take a breath before reacting. Remind yourself that the feedback you're getting is an investment in your book.

And remember, you always have veto power. If something doesn't sit right, you can say no.

2. Ask Lots of Questions

Editing is like therapy for your book: the best results come when you engage with the process.

If you don't understand a change, ask *why*. "What are you seeing here?" or "Can you walk me through this suggestion?" opens a dialogue that deepens your understanding of your own writing.

Great editors love explaining their thinking. They want you to walk away not just with a better manuscript, but with sharper instincts as a writer.

And if your editor can't explain *why* they're suggesting something, that's a red flag. Every edit should have a purpose beyond "I just think it sounds better."

3. Take Breaks Before Responding

Never reply to editorial feedback on the same day you read it.

Your first reaction is emotional ("They hated it!"). Your second reaction is rational ("Oh wait, they might have a point").

Let feedback sit for 24 hours. Go for a walk, vent to a friend, whatever it takes. Then come back with fresh eyes. Nine times out of ten, the note that initially offended you turns out to be the one that makes your book stronger.

The Ghost's Notes
This post of mine on editing went "viral" on LinkedIn:

Here's a hot take: I don't think editors should silo their work into "developmental, line, copy, or proof."

In my experience, when I see something that needs fixing, be it a misplaced comma or a broken narrative arc, I fix it. Full stop.

That's the kind of editing I want for my clients. Not a half-finished manuscript that's been "copyedited but not developmentally edited." Not a polished sentence inside a shaky chapter. But a manuscript that's genuinely ready for the next stage.

This is why I'm building a team of editors who aren't afraid to step outside their box. Yes, copyediting has its role as a final polish. But in my world, the editor isn't there to tick a service box. Great editors deliver a complete and polished manuscript that moves an author's vision forward.

I bundle this into my ghostwriting and book coaching so clients don't get nickel-and-dimed. They get what they came for: a manuscript they can be proud of.

What do you think: should editors stay in their lane, or take a more holistic approach?

By now, you've probably realized editing is less like cleaning up and more like excavating. You start with a mountain of words. You chip away at what doesn't belong. You polish what does. And if you're doing it right, you'll find your book's truest voice sitting right there in the middle, blinking up at you.

A final reminder before you move on:

You will never feel "done." Every author has to choose a moment to stop tweaking and let go.

What's the Worst That Could Happen? (Revisited)

There's a moment in every author's journey when you sit back, look at the document, and think:

What have I done?

You've spent months (years?) writing this thing. You've questioned every word, every comma, every moment of clarity. And now you're at the part that no one really prepares you for: the silence that follows finishing.

It's quieter than you expected, isn't it?

And in that quiet, an old voice tends to return. It's the very same one that followed you from the beginning.

What's the worst that could happen?

You've already lived through so many versions of that question.

You asked it when you started writing.

You asked it when you told someone about your idea.

You asked it when you shared your draft with an editor.

And now, you're asking it again as you prepare to take your book into the world.

The difference is that this time, you know the answer.

The Worst That Could Happen

The worst that could happen is that you grow.

That you learn what kind of writer you are.

That you look back at your early drafts and realize how far you've come.

The worst that could happen is that you finish what you started.

The worst that could happen is that you discover what is possible.

The Best That Could Happen

You might reach the reader who didn't know they needed you.

You might get an email that says something like "This book found me at the right time."

You might start a conversation that grows into a movement, or find collaborators who make your next project possible.

You might finally believe what everyone's been trying to tell you (me especially!): that your voice matters.

That's the best that could happen. And everything in between is what it means to live a writer's life.

The Ghost's Notes
When I started writing this book, I thought I was documenting what I already knew.

But what I've realized is that I've been learning alongside you. I've been testing, tweaking, rewriting, doubting, experimenting.

So I'll keep sharing what happens. The launches, the lessons, the moments that make me cringe, and the ones that make me proud. Because this book is just the beginning!

And if you ever find yourself drowning in doubt, just ask yourself the same question that started it all.

Your Turn

You have everything you need now.

You know how to write, plan, and edit your book.

You know how to manage the fear that will show up again (because it always does). You know how to replace gatekeeping with generosity—both for yourself and for the people who'll come to you one day asking, "How did you do it?"

When that happens, you'll smile. You'll say something like, "It started with one question."

And they'll lean in.

And you'll tell them, "I asked myself, *What's the worst that could happen?* And then I did it anyway."

What Comes After "The End"

Maybe you'll close this book and go back to your draft. Maybe you'll post your first excerpt online. Maybe you'll start outlining your next idea.

Whatever you do, keep writing. Keep choosing curiosity over certainty.

Because this isn't the end of your book journey. It's the beginning of your *author* journey.

And as far as I can tell, that's where all the best stories start.

A Note from Me

If you've made it here, thank you. Thank you for trusting me to walk beside you through the doubt, the deadlines, the drafts, and the dreams.

If you'd like to keep walking together, I'll be sharing the next chapter of this experiment—what it looks like to publish this book, market it, test new ideas, and build the next layer of the ecosystem in real time. You can find me where I always am: writing, teaching, and learning out loud.

Hold on, do you think we're DONE?!

Hate to disappoint you, but a book's journey doesn't end once the manuscript is complete! Did you think it did?

We still have a long road ahead.

If you've finished this book, it means you're ready for the next one. Check out *publish it.* to learn how to take your manuscript to market.

I'll see you there.

Get the Writing Support You Need

If you'd like ongoing support with your book-building, visit www.entrechatpress.com

And, join our author community at https://www.skool.com/write-it-with-adina-samuels-8867

What Others Are Saying

"Writing is hard for me. Real hard. Standing in front of a thousand or so people and saying virtually the same thing is much easier than writing about it. It's not that I feared it – I just didn't want to do it. But Adina broke it down for me, so it was simple. Rather than long sessions, I had shorter bursts that ultimately led to finishing the book. As Adina writes, "Finishing a book doesn't require endless hours." Small chunks add up over time. The key is to be diligent. As the saying goes, if you aim at nothing, you'll hit every time. That's why you need help developing the right path to writing a book. I figured out the hard way that going it alone didn't work. Having an editor/coach like Adina helps set goals and keep you accountable. It certainly helped me." — Bruce Dorris, Past President and CEO of the Association of Certified Fraud Examiners

"Adina is the book coach every aspiring author dreams of finding. If you've got a story to tell but it's still stuck inside you, she's like that perfect pillow - the one that cradles you just right and unlocks the deep rest you need to become the best version of yourself. She brings so much talent and passion to her craft, and she's encouraging and insightful in exactly the right ways. This is the voice that makes you believe in your story enough to WRITE IT!" — Tamara Rebick, Founder & CXO of CORIPHERY Holistic Consulting Solutions Inc.

"It is my great pleasure to work with Adina on my book project. She has a sense of what I need when it comes to finding ways to move the project forward. She sees enough light to keep me moving, even when I don't see it myself. Her authenticity (honesty, kindness, and openness) enables our work together. As a professional, she is great! As a person, even better!" — Fred Volk, Director of Doctoral Research, Liberty University

"Adina brings clarity to messy ideas, creates momentum, and builds systems that truly moves a project forward. She challenged me to articulate my "spiky opinions," giving me permission to lean into my unique point of view and hone my message for a specific audience. This book captures her coaching style perfectly. It feels like a thinking partner walking alongside you. Her approach is to support writers while holding them accountable, staying open-minded, practical, and deeply action-oriented - all while keeping things human and fun with her sense of humour." — Raelynn Douglas, CEO of Raesoleil and Co-Founder of MyLifeCatcher

About the Author

Adina Samuels is the founder of Entrechat Press, an end-to-end publishing company for first-time nonfiction authors. She has had a front-row seat to some of the world's most remarkable minds, including CEOs of Dunkin' Donuts, Cirque du Soleil, Starbucks, and TOMS Shoes.

Her work has taken her into deep conversations with Ivy League professors, *New York Times* bestselling authors, Olympians, UN officials, FBI agents, and executives from global brands like Nestlé and Airbnb. She is known for asking the questions that uncover the moments that shape people, and for helping turn those moments into stories that last.

Adina works with people who feel a pull to leave something meaningful behind. Through Entrechat Press, she helps authors shape their ideas, stories, and insights into books that carry their legacy forward.